Rev. James Rettie

From Chest to Chancel

novum pro

This book is also available as e-book.

www.novum-publishing.co.uk

© 2018 novum publishing

ISBN 978-3-99064-426-3
Editing: Hugo Chandler, BA
Cover photos: Rev. James Rettie
Cover design, layout & typesetting:
novum publishing
Internal illustrations: Rev. James Rettie

The images provided by the author
have been printed in the highest
possible quality.

www.novum-publishing.co.uk

When Jim eventually responded to the call of God on his life, he first trained as a Missionary, serving the Home Board of the Church of Scotland. That took him to places such as Easterhouse in Glasgow and later to Culloden, Inverness to establish a congregation in the Church which is now known as The Barn Church, Culloden. From there he went on to train for the ministry of Word and Sacrament. Having qualified, he had a probationary period in the Presbytery of Lanark before being called to be minister of Melness and Tongue Church in Sutherland. There he was led into the ministry of Divine Healing and after retirement this took him to places like Malawi, South Africa, India and the Congo, (DRC). This book tells of God's love, His grace and His mercy through fulfilled prophecy and answered dreams.

The reader of this book will be reminded of how God is faithful to fulfil His prophecies, keeps His promises and guides our dreams. In this book, the author, Jim, with illustrations from his own experiences reveals something of the mysterious and miraculous working of God in people's lives. It gives hope to any who may think that they cannot achieve anything in life or could never be used by God in any great way. It is a testimony to the power of God's Word to bless, to deliver and to heal people. The Bible is filled with stories of little people, limited people, and in some cases low-life people, who penetrated the barriers beyond which they thought that they dare not go, yet God used them to do amazing things. And in a way, this book is about someone like that. If you feel ill equipped, uneducated, or too old or too young, then you may be exactly the one who needs to read this book. The purpose of writing this book is to encourage people to trust in God's plan for their lives.

The author
Reverend Jim Rettie
Leader of the Christian Fellowship, Highlands, Scotland.

FROM CHEST TO CHANCEL

The word 'Chest' can mean many things, but here it refers to a 'Chest of drawers'. The 'Chancel' is the part of a Church containing the Altar or Communion Table and baptismal font in other words, the Sacramental area.

The 'Chest'

I was born in Aberdeenshire, at a place called Leochel-Cushnie, where my parents were part of the hill farming community. It was in the month of April and I am told that there was a severe snow storm at the time. We were very poor and there was no 'crib' for this babe. My bed was the bottom drawer of a chest of drawers. My mother used to often tell of how one day an old shepherd came in from tending his sheep on the hill, to see the new born 'bairn'.

Looking down at me in the bottom drawer of that chest of drawers he said in the local dialect, "Aye Jimmy Rettie one day ye'll be a minister."

Like another mother many years before, Mary, my mother nursed that prophecy in her heart, sometimes with love and hope, but at other times in rebuke. Too often, in the wild stage of my life, I would hear her say, "And to think Jimmy Rettie (she always called me Jimmy when angry with me) that old shepherd said that one day you would be a minister." So often I must have broken her heart, but she never forgot the words of that shepherd.

At an early age we moved to a farm at Dyce, on the edge of the Dyce Airfield. It was called 'Sleepy Hillock'. I don't know why it got that name as with my father around there was not much time for sleeping. My brother and I as lads were involved in grooming horses, mucking out byres, and carrying milk pails, as my mother milked the cows. No milking machines in those days. Neither were there any of the modern harvester machines of today. Hay and corn was cut by horse drawn blades or binders, with the hay being built into coles (small stacks) and the corn being thrown out of the binder as sheaves, which had to be hand stacked set up one against another in groups of six or eight. When ready the coles of hay had to be dragged to a corner of the field to be stacked.

These were exciting times for us boys. When we would gather at the field, my father would literally throw us up on top of a massive Clydesdale horse, which we had to steer to the nearest cole. The art, and there was an art to dragging coles of hay, was to attach to one side of the horse's collar (part of its harness) a chain and having led the horse around the cole, the chain was then lying at the base of the cole. We would slide off that mountain of a horse, and tuck the chain, carefully at the edge of the base of the cole and link the loose end of the chain to the other side of the horse's collar. I would then take the long reins, sit on the cole and command the horse to go, reining it towards the stacking area. More than once in a day, the chain would not be properly set and as the horse moved forward, the cole of hay would come over the top of me. As I struggled to the surface I would see the horse, faithfully, at times I think laughingly, going towards the stacking area dragging the empty chain, my father tearing his hair out. We'll say nothing about the language directed at me and the horse.

There was also the potato harvesting. In those days school children were given what was known as 'tattie holidays'; two weeks off school to help harvest potatoes grown on the local farms. That was the only time that we, along with the other kids were paid for working. One of the jobs that I disliked the most was harvesting turnips. It usually took place in wintertime and it was seen as weakness to wear gloves or mitts. You had to lift the turnip from the ground by the shaw, (stem) and with a 'tapner' (a steel blade with a wooden handle) slice off the root and the shaw, leaving the treated turnips in neat rows. Hands would become blue with the cold. Though we were working closely with nature, there was seldom any mention of God, the creator of it all. However, in reflection, I have come to believe that many of the farming community working closely with nature might not make much mention of God, but subconsciously are aware of a dependence on Him, and His order of things.

Constantly keeping an eye on the weather elements, I remember particularly my father speaking of keeping one field fallow every seven years. I never heard him say who had told him that, but I have since realised that it is according to the word of God (Exodus; Chapter 23; Verses 10 and 11). Other than the essential care of the animals, no work was done on a Sunday.

School Days

We had to walk three miles to get to the nearest school, which was at Overton. It was a one classroom school with one teacher, Miss Robertson, having to teach pupils from ages five to twelve. In that time there were no calculators or computers. Most of our work in the early stages was done with chalk on slates. I would have to confess that I was not too excited about school. I remember the lovely big wood fire for heating the room and I always had an interest in the bottle of milk and sandwiches that we each had to take with us as lunch.

Miss Robertson was a lovely person and she must have had an amazing brain and memory to teach across such a range of subjects and age groups and an unending measure of patience in coping with us all. To help her keep order she had a large black strap which she kept in a drawer in her desk. I can testify to her readiness to use it.

On one particular occasion, I cannot recall exactly the cause of the offence, but I think that it was something that happened on the way to or from School. Teacher decided that it warranted three of the best. My hands were well hardened with the work I did, but she seemed to delight in making sure that the leather contacted the wrist area, which was most painful. I was so mad at her, that the next morning I was at school early. I took the belt from the drawer and I stuck it in the blazing fire. I thought that that would be the end of that. But during the day she had discovered the loss and she did not need a crystal bowl to realise who the culprit was. Going next door to her house, she returned with what seemed like an even bigger belt, and meted out six of the best, three on each hand, and wrist.

Whilst I didn't have much interest in text books, I do recall enjoying picture books, especially the Bible stories – Moses and the Red Sea – Daniel in the Lions' Den – Samson and such characters. And of course we had our daily Bible reading and the Lord's Prayer. With us being about three miles from the nearest church, that was the only Bible teaching that we had. At home, if the Name of our Lord was mentioned, it was in vain. Even Christmas was just another day, with our Santa out of season at the New Year. A stocking containing a piece of coal at the toe, an orange or an apple, maybe a pencil or a jotter.

About every six months, the Minister would call around in his pony and trap, doing his rounds. I recall that he had a particular interest in what we boys had caught in our traps. Most nights we would set traps (snares) to catch rabbits and pheasants and such. Mostly, we would take them down to the Big House at Stoneywood, about four miles away, or we would sell them to the butcher when he came around with his van, as did the baker. That was our pocket money. Of course the Minister, on his visits would get a gift from our traps. I am sure that the bountiful Lord provided well for His servant on those rural visits as he would return home with eggs, cheeses, hens, rabbits, potatoes and such. But he was not neglecting his Kingdom work, having encouraged our parents to have us children baptised.

My sister having been born, there were now three of us. The Minister did a home baptism and that was us done, aged eleven, ten and three. There was one person whom I think had an influence on my young mind; he was an old sailor who came to stay in the farm 'bothy' and to work on the farm. We called him Pop Jennings. We would listen for ages to the many fascinating stories that he told of his travels and his adventures in many different countries. I think that sparked an interest in me to travel and see other countries.

The Airfield

In reflection, life was much of a mystery and an adventure for we boys, especially living so near to the airfield, which we saw go from a grass landing area to tarred runways and to a fully operational airfield. For a country boy, it was exciting to see and at times to be involved in all that was going on. It was a mystery to see and to hear people of different colours and dialects. It was more so when some German prisoners of war came and had their 'holding billets' in an area behind the farm. Every morning and evening they would be marched, with guards, to and from the canteen for their meals.

Dyce Airfield was one of the targets of Germany and there were constant air raids to try to bomb and to destroy it. Its main protection was that the airfield was nestled in the shadow of a stone quarry. The raiding aircraft crossing that way were over the airfield before they could see it and were then over the city of Aberdeen, which was next in line. The downside of that was that Aberdeen suffered from constant bombing raids.

On one occasion we were awakened with the cattle in the front garden and we learned that an unexploded bomb had landed in one of the fields with the impact knocking down part of the dyke and gate, allowing the cattle to escape. It was thought that one pilot had been returning from a raid on Aberdeen, realised that he still had one bomb on board and just jettisoned it. We didn't mind, because the field was near the road to school and it took about a fortnight for them to defuse and to remove it, during which time we were not allowed to go to school. Being near the Airfield was for us a great adventure, because when the air raid siren sounded all sorts of vehicles; trucks and mobile anti-aircraft guns would come out from the camp and line up on the roadway past the farm. We, as boys, would join the Royal Air Force (RAF) men and women sheltering under the vehicles. I still can't fathom the reasoning, but it was believed that being under those vehicles was the safest place to be at such a time. What I do know is that under those vehicles we as boys heard and saw things which were an advanced education for life. Through it all we got to know some of the 'Boys in Blue' quite well and we even got involved in some camp activities.

The camp football pitch was on one of the farm fields and they would tell us when a game was to be played. We would go down and move any cattle or sheep that were there on to another field. I think some of them adopted my brother and me as mascots, encouraged us to 'kick about with them', at times involving us in their training sessions. They gave me the name 'Little Hooky'. I don't know if that was because I was good at 'hooking' their heels in order to trip them, or more likely that it was a particular skill I had for 'hooking' a ball into the goalmouth area, for the striker to hit it home for a goal. The experience certainly fired up for me an interest in the game of football, which stayed with me for a major part of my life.

I think that I was about eleven years of age when my father had a serious accident to his hand, with a circular saw, when cutting wood and we decided to give up farm work. As a family we moved into the village of Dyce. Compared to what it is now, it was very small and basic. For me, it meant a change of school; not a happy experience. I think that I was seen as a backwoods boy and was made fun of by some of the street wise boys. Being quite self-conscious, that affected me quite badly and may have been the cause of my becoming a bit rebellious in trying to compensate for it. I thought that my contribution to the school football team would help me to be accepted, but that raised some degree of jealousy.

I joined the Boys' Brigade, mainly because I had heard that there was the chance of playing football for the team. I would have to admit that I missed the spiritual importance of the B.B. and I had no sense of learning and serving the Lord. I am sure that the captain and the officers did their best but it did not touch me. My main interest was in football and that was greatly encouraged. May I say that over the years, having been involved at all different levels within the Boys' Brigade movement, I have the highest respect for the work that they do for the Kingdom.

Age rather than qualification moved my schooling to Bankhead Senior Secondary (now Bankhead Academy) which was about three miles away from Aberdeen. I had little or no interest in the academic subjects, but I enjoyed woodwork and I had an interest in becoming a joiner. But my main interest was football and I played for the school team. Many of my Saturdays consisted of playing for the school team in the morning. playing for the Boys' Brigade in the afternoon and often the village team in the evening. Some of the pitches in Aberdeen were cinder pitches. I think that they got the cinders as waste fuel from the Gas Works, which were spread and rolled to make an even surface. Even, but very abrasive if you went down. I continued my interest in the RAF camp and I persuaded the local newsagent to allow me to sell Sunday papers at the Camp. That graduated to selling cigarettes and that led me to start smoking – those were the days of 'Willie Woodbines' or the more classy 'Senior Service', 'Capstan', 'Passing Clouds', 'Craven A 'and 'Gold Flake' and when unavailable, I would smoke cinnamon sticks. How desperate can one get?

By the time I had left school at fifteen years of age, with no qualifications, I was smoking a lot and drinking alcohol quite regularly. Any thoughts of being a joiner were 'out the window', but I needed to find work. My search led me again back to the RAF Station, where I began work with the Navy, Army, Air Force. Institution (NAAFI) as a message boy, with the intention of becoming a grocer. That opened wider the door of opportunity for me to indulge in smoking and drinking. With so many young women around, it was all too easy to get involved with the opposite sex. Sadly, for many young people today, that is a normal life style, but in those days, it was seen as being a bit crazy. My mother must have recognised that.

One day when I was about seventeen years old, she said, "It's time that you boys went up to see the Minister and joined the Church."

We weren't too hurried to do that, but she persevered and she found out when the 'Communicants' Classes were due to start. To please her we decided to have a look and to see what and who else was to be involved. As we watched from a distance we saw some rather attractive girls going into the church and I think that swayed us to give it a go. We faithfully did the course and we got the certificate, but the teaching, which I am sure was done well, had little effect on me and I continued with my life, smoking, drinking, dancing and romancing and of course, I was still playing football.

National Service

Though the Second World War had ended; young men were still being called up to do what was known as their National Service. This meant that they had to, unless exempt for health or work reasons, spend at least two years in one of the armed forces. I had hoped that my work with the NAAFI, who provide a service to the armed forces throughout the world, would exempt me from 'call up', but no! Faced with that prospect I had two things in mind; a) I would want to be in the RAF and b) I would want to serve abroad. On meeting with the relevant authorities, I made my requests known, only to learn that they were full up with candidates for National Service in the RAF, and they would only consider those who would agree to serve for a term longer than two years. The opportunity to serve overseas would be more available for anyone who decided to serve for three or more years. So, there it was, I decided to sign on for three years in the RAF. That led to three months 'square bashing' (Basic Training) at Bridge North, England, followed by two months in transit camp at Lytham St. Anne's, near Blackpool, at the height of summer. It seemed like paradise for a young man in Air Force Blues. Our destination was the Second Tactical Air Force, stationed at Oldenburg in Germany, where there was a squadron of Hunter Jets to be kept operational. I was there for the rest of my National service.

I had great plans to take the opportunity of getting some academic qualifications, also to learn to drive and to speak the German Language. But the lure of the German social life, with bars open most of the night and a more liberal style of social life was too much of a temptation, and my understanding of the language was limited to that area of life. My other interest of course, was football and I found myself playing for the Equipment Section, where I worked, and also for the station team. That took me to other Stations throughout Germany and also to some German stadiums. In that, I was excused many of the mundane duties like parades and guard duties. Though we were no longer at war with Germany there was a certain intensity in keeping those Hunter Jets in service. I was involved in making sure that there were sufficient bits and pieces to maintain them. Doing that I graduated to the rank of corporal. When I was due to return to the UK and be demobbed, the Squadron Leader at the time, tried to persuade me to sign on for another term, offering me a third stripe, and an extended tour in Germany. But I felt that I was too much of a free thinker to continue in that rather rigid and disciplined life and I told him that it was not for me.

Back in Civvy Street

I became an employee of Lipton's Grocery chain, working in the Union Street branch in Aberdeen. I learned to drive and that added to the pace of my life; and whatever car I had, or drove, my aim seemed to be to push it to its maximum. As I graduated to the bigger and the faster cars, I began to get a reputation as a fast driver. Unlike today, not many young people had cars, but those who did were always up for a challenge to race one another. Of course, I quickly got back into my old style of life, playing football for local teams, spending time in the bars and going to dances. In those days, most villages held what was known as a Gala Day or Week. Part of the attraction was Five-a-side Football matches, with the final being on the Saturday night. I was playing at one in a place called Logie Durno, twenty-five miles from Aberdeen and afterwards there was the usual Marque Dance.

It was there that I met a young woman called Pearl who was from Fyvie. To me she was as the one sung about in the Scottish song 'The Bonnie Lass O' Fyvie'. She was a lovely quiet, gentle country girl, but soon she became caught up in my crazy life style. What did that look like? Well, Friday night would be spent in some bar, mostly playing darts for drinks and I was quite good at that. Then on Saturday night, we would arrange to go to some dance, mostly in the country and as I had a big Austin sixteen car, I was usually the driver. I would start off in the Stoneywood Bar, and after a few drinks I would set off for Fyvie where I would collect Pearl and the others, then we would set off for the dancing, which could be another twenty to thirty miles away.

After a night's dancing, I would drive Pearl and the others home, then at some hour in the middle of the night, make my way home. On Sunday, I would again be on my way out to Fyvie, and often I ended up at the British Legion, for an evening of drinking before returning home. How crazy was that! No thought of God, or church.

At such times, I can still hear my mother saying with shock and disappointment in her voice, "And to think Jimmy Rettie, that old shepherd said that one day you would be a minister!" She always called me Jimmy Rettie when she was angry or disappointed with me.

In the midst of all that, I do believe that Pearl had a good influence in my life. We got engaged and were married in the Church at Fyvie where Pearl was a member. We had no house in which to start our married life, so we got ourselves a small residential caravan which we were allowed to park in the corner of a 'corn yard' at a farm at Bucksburn, which was four miles north from Aberdeen. It was an unsettled time for me. I had left my grocery job, to drive a bakery van, selling bakery and grocery goods around the streets. After about eighteen months, I gave that up and went into partnership in a furniture business, often driving a furniture van, delivering furniture to areas like Wick and Thurso. Though married, my lifestyle had not changed much, and I messed up in that business.

We then moved to a flat in Aberdeen where I took a job with a Credit Warehouse Firm in Aberdeen with regular collections being made in the Huntly, Keith areas, which meant travelling on the Glens of Foudland most days. Though I was at the age when most people have gathered some sense, I must still have been seen as a 'loose cannon'. The evidence for that is in the following.

It was the day of my brother's wedding, at which I was to be Best Man. It was on a Saturday and I had to make a business run to Huntly, twenty-five miles North of Aberdeen. To make sure I behaved myself and got back in time, it was arranged that my 'Namesake' uncle would accompany me. Our vehicle for the day was a small Austin Van. I did the business and I persuaded my uncle that we should have a couple of beers before setting off home. Of course, that made us somewhat late and my uncle made sure that the wedding company knew all about it, as he shared the following story.

"We left Huntly in great haste, with Jim overtaking everything else on the road. At one point he overtook this car. I looked in the rear window mirror and I saw the driver open his door and step out. Jim had passed him at such a speed that the man thought that his car had stopped."

I made the wedding on time and I performed my brotherly duty. Then came the news of Pearl being with child and that should have been a sobering influence on me, but about that time I changed my job yet again. I think I used the addition to the family with Pearl having to stop her job of work, as the excuse for the change, believing that I could make more money. The job was a 'direct selling job'. It was high risk as it paid commission only, if you didn't sell you didn't earn. The company was Siemens, the product was a multi-purpose vacuum cleaner. I felt confident in my ability to sell things, wondering why it was so easy to get a job with such high commission. It seemed to be the challenge that I needed. But the blinkers came off very quickly when I met the other salespeople. They were mostly, but not all, ex-cons and social rejects. Unknown to me at the time, direct selling jobs were mostly taken up by people who could not get other jobs. My concern was how easily I identified with them and I felt at home in their company. I was given a place on a team of six or seven men with one as supervisor. In the morning we would be taken to and dropped off in the area to be canvassed. From ten a.m. till two p.m. we would knock on doors and try and persuade people to have a demonstration of our wonderful machine. The demonstration was arranged for the evening when, hopefully both husband and wife would be at home.

At about six p.m., armed with a demonstration model, we were dropped off by the supervisor at our arranged demos. I enjoyed doing the demonstrations, possibly because I believed that it was a great machine, though in the end it was just a vac. But in the demos, we exaggerated its ability to the extent that it sounded as if it could do all but comb your hair and brush your teeth. There were no mobile phones then, so we had to have certain signals to keep in touch with the supervisor. Whilst unpacking the machine we would ask the customer if it was okay to put a certain part of the packaging in the window to let the boss know where we were. Then, if, after the demo they had agreed to purchase the machine and I had the deal signed and sealed, I would ask if I could change the sign to another part of the packaging to let the boss know that I was ready for my next demo. As he drove around the various demo areas he would see it and collect me. However, if I was struggling to close a deal, I would ask the same question, but this time I would use another part of the packaging which was the signal that I was struggling to close. Then the supervisor would appear and as well as collecting me he would add his weight of persuasion to press the customer to purchase. Mostly, we offered to take their present vacuum in part exchange to help with the deposit. So he would ask me what I offered for the part exchange.

I would tell him, and with a mock look of surprise he would say, "Oh I think we could do better than that," and he would make a higher offer that was likely to reduce my commission, but well, a little is better than nothing.

If that didn't swing it he would change tack with no holds barred – mostly the wife was interested, but the husband was not. After pressing home the attributes of the machine to 'spray paint' or oil spray the underside of the car and of course it could be adapted to be used to drive a saw and if that didn't work, it would come down to something like this.

"Your wife loves it, don't you dear? Think how much easier it would make her life and how clean the carpets would be for the children crawling." The final thing, "Don't you think that your wife is worth it?" Well, you hold your breath after that one. But often it worked.

From my side, the setup was that I was paid a high commission on every sale made, less that given for the part exchange machine, which the company had a listed price for, or I could re-sell it myself if I got a better deal. It was all about money. The supervisor got commission on every machine sold by his team. As there was no basic pay, the pressure to sell was great. I would have to confess that I was not proud of often persuading people to buy something that they did not need; and often could not afford.

Anyhow, I must have been good at it because within three weeks I was promoted to supervisor and got a team of my own. They numbered between five and six, with a constant turnover and they were a wild bunch. They were given basic details of the qualities of the machine and instructions on the art of demonstrating it to advantage, then more or less handed a machine. The vehicles used by the company were ten-seater Commer Dormobile type, which were said to be the fastest commercial vehicles on the road at the time. I still believe that. Being a country boy at heart, I began taking the team out into the country villages. At first, they were not too pleased about that as it meant longer hours and less comforts. But later they came to realise that country folk at that time did not have so many household gadgets; they were careful with their cash and had a little to spare. They were less resistant to pressure, if not a little gullible and we did very well. Some of the team had no scruples in persuading people to purchase our machine, and at times one of them would seem to be lost.

I would eventually find that he was settling the deposit in the bedroom. I still feel a sense of shame when I think of some of the tactics that I used in closing sales for some of the team. The result was that there was a lot of cash around. Some of the team seemed to have a burning need to spend it. And somehow, we got access to what I would call a friendly hotel in the town, whose back door was open to the team at any hour of the day or night. Much time and money was spent there.

Friday nights were particularly outrageous. We would usually finish early and sometimes met up with the other teams working in the area; the Cockit Hat Pub was a favourite haunt. Most of the time members of my team were single, and they would party outrageously, with little thought to time or consequences. More than once we were barred from the place. The police knew about us. Twice I was caught and convicted for speeding and though there were not the same strict rules regarding drunk driving, as there are now (breathalysers and such), I still don't know why I was never caught and charged with drunk driving, especially on my trips to Edinburgh which was a weekly thing.

As supervisor, I had to get the part exchange machines back to the depot in Edinburgh and collect a stock of new ones. It became a Sunday routine. Just after teatime, I would meet some of the team at the office. We would load the old machines, then adjourn to the 'local' bar next door. After a few drinks I would get into the vehicle at about ten o'clock and set off for Edinburgh, full speed as usual. There were no A90s or A9s (cell phones) in those days. I would arrive in Edinburgh in the early hours of the morning, having arranged for someone to meet me at the depot. We would then unload the old and load the new. I would then put my head down in the vehicle until about six or seven a.m., then I would set off for Aberdeen to meet the team at ten a.m. to put them on the selected streets to canvas for demonstrations. I would then go home and get my head down until it was time to collect the team at two p.m.

Returning from one of those trips, I was coming over the hill towards Forfar when, too late, I spotted a police car, which signalled me to stop. Turning down my window, I waited for him to approach me. The conversation went something like this.

Me, "Good Morning Constable, is there something wrong? Was I travelling too fast?"

Constable, "No! No! you were just flying too low!"

The result was that at the subsequent court case, I got a hefty fine and had my licence taken away from me for a year.

Home Front

Whilst all this was going on I had my loving, devoted and ever-so-patient wife at home, caring for our daughter June. We were blessed with caring neighbours who were there for them when I was not. During week-days we were like ships passing in the night, but weekends were special, when I possibly over-compensated for my guilty conscience. Of course, there was the matter of having June Baptised. With both of us being 'members' of the Church we felt that we had the right to receive baptism for our child. And though our involvement in the Church was only for 'hatches' (baptisms), 'matches', (weddings) and 'despatches' (funerals), we found a minister who agreed to do the baptism in his Church.

The reason why I became involved in direct selling was for the big money. I was at that time earning what would have been thought of as big money; but my lifestyle made a sizeable drain on it, so the difficulty of budgeting for home needs was left to Pearl. I am still amazed at how she managed that so well. How true are those words of the Bible where it says, *"Whoever loves money, never has money enough, whoever loves wealth is never satisfied with his income. As goods increase, so do those who consume them.* (Ecclesiastes; Chapter 5; Verses 11 and 12).

But now with no driving licence my job and my income were at risk. However, the company were sympathetic. They allowed me to continue as a supervisor if I arranged for and paid a driver. Well, that was better than nothing, so though it was not ideal, I went for it. What added to the frustration at the time was that I was being regularly 'head hunted' by other direct-selling companies. But when they learned that I had no driving licence that was the end of it. Then the company came up with the request that I consider moving to Edinburgh, to become the working manager of the Edinburgh Branch. That would involve managing at least four teams, and supervising one. The bonus would be that they would provide and pay for a driver for me. It would mean leaving Pearl and baby June in Aberdeen, seeing them only once a month. The 'package' seemed good, the money was great, and I suppose that it appealed to my sense of adventure.

So, I landed in Edinburgh, living in bed and breakfast accommodation. The teams consisted of much the same type, but except for one or two, there was less of the wild streak in them. It is one of the things that I noticed about Edinburgh folk; the most extreme of them would have an air of order or respect lurking in them. I had a gem of a driver. He enjoyed the weekend runs we had to Aberdeen. Despite one or two unruly 'blips' we did well. The Company were pleased, the teams enjoyed some healthy competition, and some big money, and for me, it was a good time. Then I got my driving licence back. And at about the same time there was trouble at the Glasgow Branch, and I was asked to become manager of the Glasgow office. Again the 'package' was attractive, and so I landed-up in Glasgow. And I quickly discovered that the teams I had in Aberdeen were tame compared with what I had in Glasgow.

Again, I reflect on how easily I seemed to get alongside those lads, and get drawn into their way of life. Direct selling was beginning to open up in a greater way, with Encyclopaedias, and other Vac Machines, and the pressure to sell was even greater. And often I would get caught up with one of the team in persuading some couple that our machine was far superior to their almost new Vac, and pressurise them to do a part exchange for a machine that they did not need and could not afford. And of course, at the end of the day or week, there was much bragging and toasting to those things.

And to give an idea of what that often involved, I relate two happenings in particular. One was at the end of a Friday night of celebration in a Bar in the Govan area of Glasgow, when two of the team, in very high spirits (from a bottle) decided to do a dance on the roof and bonnet of a car which was sitting outside the Bar. We had to make a speedy exit from that area.

The second was when, again on a Friday night we were returning from Coatbridge, outside Glasgow. On passing a farm, we saw floodlights and some sort of celebration going on. The cry went up from the team, "Stop!" Stop!, Let's join in." On doing so, we discovered that it was a barn dance. We were welcomed to join in. There was of course ample provision of drink to be had and the team seemed to be making up for lost time.

In the early hours of the morning I was called from the dance floor, to go outside. There, I found one of the team facing up to what I took to be a local lad and each had a pitch fork in their hand. To add to the scene there was a young woman, wringing her hands and pleading with them to stop. Now, I had often used a pitch fork for its proper use, but I knew how lethal a weapon those two-pronged forks could be, had I not stabbed many a rat with one?

The word spread and people started pouring out of the barn, with the playground like cry, "A fight! A fight!" and recognising that there were more of them than of us, it was time to make a hasty retreat, so with the cry, "To the wagon!" we somehow got out of there.

The shock of the incident must still have been with me when I drove into Glasgow heading for the office in Hope Street. The street was empty, which was unusual, even at that hour, when all at once I was faced with a sea of lights racing towards us. I realised that the traffic lights had changed and that I was driving up the wrong way in a one-way street. With flashing lights and blaring horns the Glasgow night life raced past us in my stationary panic. Then the Blue lights appeared. Speaking to the policeman through the window, I tried to put on my Aberdeen accent, claimed that I was a stranger in town and that I didn't know the streets.

Looking in the back and hearing the careless hilarity of the team, he said, "Are you all Aberdeen lads?"

With a note of hope mixed with despair, I said, "Aye we are."

With that he turned to his colleague and said, "Come on," and the two of them with arms spread, stood facing the new wave of oncoming traffic, whilst over his shoulder he shouted, "Get out of here!"

A sharp U turn saw me back on the right way. Unknown to me at the time was that that was the start of another U turn, which was to change my life. Before going on to that, I would like to say that the Glasgow Bobbies are great. Not because we got off that time, but because of my experience of them in major incidents, I would back them against the most threatening force. Of course many of them were, and may still be, men from the Highlands.

During my time in Glasgow I seldom had, or took, the opportunity of going home. It was putting a big strain on our marriage. I think that I came to realise that without Pearl's common sense and realistic approach to things, I was going further and further down the road of a wasted life. With that in mind I arranged to rent a room from a lovely elderly widow woman in the West End of Glasgow where Pearl and June could come and stay with me. That was indeed a stabilising influence, to the effect that I decided to give up direct selling and get a normal job, with normal hours. For some time I worked in a furniture shop in Glasgow city centre. Later I went on to work for a Falkirk company who dealt in women's fashions and soft household goods. The work involved supplying stock to housewives who had been encouraged to have a 'Club' sort of industry in their home. They, in turn, encouraged their neighbours and friends to buy from them on a credit system. For that I had a purpose built van. Most of my agents were in the housing schemes in the East End of Glasgow; Easterhouse, Garthamlock and out at Coatbridge. At that time those places had a rather bad reputation and towards the end of some days I would be carrying quite a sum of money, apart from the value of the van stock, yet I never once sensed that I was at any risk.

Whilst travelling about the East End, I heard of a flat for rent, just off London Road. It wasn't in the most attractive area, but it had two rooms, a small kitchen and bathroom, so we moved into it. The owner of the flat, after her husband had died went to stay with her sister in Ayr and she tried to visit, or to check on us about once a month. She was a Christian and she let you know that she was. She would tell us stories about how God had blessed her, especially at the time of her husband's death, and how God provided for her in such amazing ways. Even now, I remember one particular story she told.

"It was after my husband had died. I was sitting in this very flat one afternoon, and I had nothing in the cupboard for tea, breakfast or lunch and I wondered where my next bite would come from, but I prayed, trusting in God," she said. "At Mid-afternoon there was a knock at the door and there standing was a person I had not seen for some time, who said 'You came into my mind today and I just brought along these few things for you'. It was provision for more than one meal." Her concluding statement of faith was something like this, "You see, if you trust God He will never let you down, so I have no fear of the future."

I believe it was her telling of those stories about God's provision that prompted Pearl to visit the Church which was just around the corner in Helmsdale Street. After a few visits she heard that they had a Young Women's Group, led by Betty Wilson, whose husband was the Boys' Brigade Captain. So, Pearl joined the Young Women's Group, later becoming an Officer in the Boys' Brigade, leading the Junior section. Part of the remit of the Young Women's Group. was to raise funds for the work of the Church. For that purpose they would, every other month, hold a dance in the Church Hall. Now that was of more interest to me than attending Church, so I willingly went along, after all it was for a good cause. There I was introduced to George Wilson, who, though I did not know it at the time, was to be my Barnabas, (my encourager). George had, and still has, a wonderful sense of the Glasgow type of humour, and he can see and poke fun at anything, in the nicest way. He had a lively sense of adventure and so many 'way out' idea. I found it to be interesting, if not a little challenging to be around him.

George didn't push religion at you, but you could not have any length of conversation with him about anything, without becoming aware that he had a close relationship with God and had a love for the Church. Whatever subject we were on, you were left thinking, *'I didn't think God had an input or interest in that'*, sometimes the most mundane things. I came to know the truth of that.

Learning of my experience as a salesperson, George began sharing his ideas with me about fund raising. One of them was to have a sale or return outlet for small household items, such as soap, dusters, talcum powder, washing up liquid, and disinfectants and such. There just happened to be a small room in the Church that was converted into what became known as the 'Sunday Shop', which members of the congregation visited after the Service. As I was in charge of the venture, I had to be there at Church every Sunday; God's ways are certainly strange. The Minister at the time, John Young, was a very tall man and very academic in his presentation of the Gospel. With the height of the pulpit and his own height you truly had the sense that he was more than the ten feet above contradiction. I could make nothing of his sermons, they went right over my head. But after all, I was there only to raise funds for them.

Another idea that George had was to have a Gala Day for the Church and community. He made maximum use of my talent as an organiser. Gala Days became annual events; one I remember had the theme 'Dr. Dolittle'. We decorated floats with models of all the animals, and things and with a band playing we paraded down to a local school, which we hired for the day. There in the playground and classrooms we had such a variety of stalls and all the fun of the fair. Those events were seen as quite a spectacle in the East End of Glasgow at that time, but I don't think it brought much increase to the Church congregation.

For myself, I felt quite comfortable with the social side of the Church activities, I may even have thought that is what the Church is all about. Again, persuaded by George, I became involved with the Boys' Brigade, especially on the football front. Before I knew it, I found myself persuaded to be the cook at one of their holiday camps at Whitley Bay, in England. By the grace of God they all survived the ordeal. Whilst being involved in those and other areas of Church activities, I always made it clear that I was willing to help in whatever way possible, but that I was having nothing to do with the spiritual side.

You can then understand our surprise when one Friday night the minister knocked on the door of our flat. I remember that he expressed his surprise and pleasure at finding a couple at home together on a Friday night in that area. It is just as well he didn't know that I was about to go across the road to Flynn's Pub for a pint. If he had, he may not have asked the question which the purpose of his visit was. He asked if I would consider becoming an elder in the Church. I explained to him that I had no leaning towards the spiritual matters of the Church, so it would not be right for me to join the court of elders. That argument didn't seem to have much effect on him. He was not prepared to take no for an answer, but that I should give it serious thought. I still have a sense of shame that having been given an invitation to such a privileged position, I found myself doing the serious thinking with a pint of beer in hand at Flynn's Bar. That was the state of play with me at the time. I knew that George would have an interest in all of this, but I knew that with him being teetotal, that he would not be in the pub, encouraging me to respond in the positive. But he wasn't far away. When I returned home, George was there waiting for me. You know, I do think God gangs up on people at times. Well, it worked, and I became an elder, but I made it clear to them all that I was not in it for the spiritual side. A bit of the Frank Sinatra there, "I did it my way". That is just how it was to be with me, or so I thought, but God had other plans.

On the home front, there were some major changes. Most Christians will have come to learn that when you turn to follow the Way of the Lord, the enemy, that old serpent the Devil, is not happy and becomes very active in trying to hinder you. That is a truth we soon discovered as we got word that the person who owned the flat we rented had decided to sell it. We couldn't afford to buy it, so we were to be homeless. To add to all that, Pearl learned that she was expecting our second child. I have since learned that the Word calls for us 'to rejoice in every situation', but wait a minute, even in all this? Haven't you more than often said that? But God is faithful to His Word and as our landlady once said, "He will provide."

I think it was the flat that came first, just across the road, above Flynn's Pub. It was one floor up, on a landing shared by two families, with a shared toilet (cludgie) on the stairs. It was rough. Ten people lived in the flat next door, the lino on the stairs was worn, broken and dangerous. The cludgie defies description. What were we to do? Well, I called on our ideas man, George.

Whilst viewing and discussing the situation, he said, "Let's do it up."

With that, the plan was made, the necessary materials bought, members of the Boys' Brigade roped in and we set about it. One weekend it was the flat, painted, papered and curtained. The second it was the cludgie, which was transformed, plastered, painted, even a curtain and lino, matching the new lino on the stair. The transformation was such that some of the children next door would invite their friends up to see their deluxe cludgie. You know, that the family respected what had been done and took their share in keeping it that way. The reason why I tell that story is that there is a message in it. When we, as Christians raise the 'Bar', whatever situation we find ourselves in, it encourages others to do likewise. The regular visit from mice running across the living room in the quiet of the evening was not too much of a disturbance. But then the discovery that Pearl was pregnant, with the prospect of bringing a baby into that situation threw us a bit. We would have to wait and see about that.

It was in March 1969 we had the new arrival, another daughter, whom we named Angela, sister to June. Plans had to be made for Angela to be baptised, which Mr Young was pleased to officiate at. Whilst I still had difficulty in understanding his sermons, I recall that on that day, as Pearl and I stood at the 'Baptismal Font' presenting our child for baptism, and confessing Christ as Lord and Saviour of our lives, something peculiar happened; much more than words could convey. At the time I still didn't understand it, but I now realise that it was the Holy Spirit confirming in my mind and in my heart that glorious message of salvation – that Jesus truly died for my sins, that by accepting Him as Lord and Saviour I am washed clean in His Blood. Praise God. I didn't get much time to rejoice and to work out what it was all about, as the next day I learned that the company I worked for decided to stop trading, so I was going to be unemployed. That old enemy at work again. Since then I have come to believe that God has a purpose in allowing the Devil to work in those times and ways, and that it is to strengthen one's faith.

At this time John Young, the Minister had retired and so we were very involved with the vacancy procedure. We quite quickly got a new minister. At one Kirk Session Meeting (when the elders meet with the Minister), the elder who was the Stewardship and Budget representative for the congregation announced that he was moving from the area. There was a call for someone to volunteer to take his place as the Steward and Budget Representative. The Minister didn't know much about me and he proposed that I take on the job of Stewardship and Budget Promoter. I think George, who was then session clerk, was behind that idea. Though I had been touched by the grace of God, I still allowed that feeling that because of my past, I was not good enough. Making clear my views, I fervently refused.

But George in his persuasive way said, "Jim, there is nothing to it. We send your name through to head office in Edinburgh, who periodically sends you leaflets etc., and you just put them on the pews for people to read and to respond to as they feel led; there is nothing to it." Put that way it seemed fairly safe, so I agreed to have my name put forward as the promoter for the congregation.

Shortly after that, I received confirmation from the Church of Scotland's Head Office in Edinburgh, along with an invitation to attend a training course. It was to be a weekend course, at a place called Gean House, at Alloa. Realising that there was to be more to this than was spoken of at the Kirk Session Meeting, I thought that I had better find out what I had gotten myself into. With no greater enthusiasm than that, I booked in for the course.

As the weekend progressed with the fellowship and the lectures, I could not get caught up in the enthusiasm of some of the others. By Sunday lunch time I had more or less decided what I was to do with all the information, which was not a lot. I wouldn't bother with all the 'Promotion Material' on offer, I would just do it my way. Most of the lectures were given by Reverend Matheson. who was at the time Minister at the Church of Scotland, at Portree in Isle of Skye. In his final talk he was giving a word of encouragement and guidance as how best to meet the challenges of that which we were taking on. I had heard and given many such promotion talks to sales teams and I was only half listening, as they say.

Then I heard him say, "Now some of you may find that your journey with the Lord is like a ladder you are climbing, you get up a few rungs, then slip back. Up again and again slip back." Then he uttered words which were life changing for me. He said, "Why don't you look up to the top of the ladder. There you will see God reaching down to draw you up. Put your hands in His hands and you will never slip back."

My mind said to me *'That's you, he is speaking to you'.* It was as if some great energy lifted me up, I felt a lightness that is not easy to explain, my whole perspective changed. Whatever goal it was that I had been aiming, struggling, battling for; all seemed pointless, I could never achieve it, *"All pointless as it says in the Book of Ecclesiastes."* All that I had heard over the weekend came to make sense; true life begins with God. He has already given us all that we need for a full life.

We find that truth in the words of the Saviour Jesus Christ who said, *"I came that they may have life and have it in all its fullness. (John 10 verse 10).*

At that moment, my whole perspective changed, and I couldn't get enough of the posters and the Visual Aids which were recommended for lively presentations. At the time I drove a little Morris Minor (bought for twenty-five pounds and I still have the receipt) and on the home journey it was pretty well full of Stewardship and Budget promotional material, and the driver with a new song in his heart; praising the Lord.

I couldn't wait to tell that man who said, "There's nothing to it" that there was everything to it. At the next Kirk Session meeting

I had the opportunity to tell the rest of the elders and to present to them the plans for a Stewardship and Budget campaign. I was in full flight, pointing out that we give because God first gave to us – our very lives – our daily provision – He gave us His only Beloved Son to die for us – He has opened up the gateway to glory for us.

When one of the elders interjected saying, "Wait a minute Jim, that sounds like Bible punching!!" there were more than one of the others who seemed to agree, with quiet, "Ayes", like you do when in a group you confess to something you know that you shouldn't be saying. I would have to confess that I was momentarily stopped in my tracks, but with a degree of determination I went on and laid the plan.

As a result of the ensuing discussion, it was decided that only those who agreed with the plan of campaign would be expected to take part. I believe it was the Holy Spirit who gave me direction to make that stand. I have since found that when involved in some great work for the Lord, it is less of a trial if you have with you people of like mind (Faith). Jesus knew and had practiced that when He raised Jairus's daughter from death (Mark; Chapter 5; Verse 35ff). Later, as I thought about what happened in the meeting, I had difficulty understanding why Elders, with concern for the spiritual welfare of the congregation would speak against teaching the Gospel. Then I thought how taken aback they must have been, finding this man who wanted to have nothing to do with spiritual things was now afire with the Spirit. We all had a lot to learn about the workings of God. The campaign which was carried out in the parish was a great success, with numbers being added to the congregation and some more pennies to the purse. Praise be to God for His faithfulness.

On the Job Front

I began working for a retail company that sold just about everything from a fur coat to a scrubbing brush. A modern-day Selfridges, except that they were suppliers as well as retailers. And for the former, they employed what were known as 'travellers'; people who visited retail outlets with samples and catalogues to encourage the buyers to place orders of the stock available at cost price. Each of the 'travellers' had what was called a journey, which was an area with the outlets for which they were responsible. Initially, I was appointed to one of those 'journeys', but soon after that, I was asked to organise what became known as 'Trade Shows'. The idea was to book a large hall or a hotel for two or three days; places where stock could be displayed and catalogues viewed. These Trade Shows were held mostly in the far reaches of the North and South of the country, involved one or two furniture vans to transport the goods and five or six staff to promote it. They were interesting and challenging occasions.

Then one day someone came into the store and bought loads of dishes; cups, saucers, plates and bowls, heaps of cutlery and pots and pans. When asked what they were for, he said that he was equipping some caravans that he was going to be letting out and indicated that others were looking at doing the same. The stock manager told that to the boss. The result was that for the next two summers I found myself visiting caravan sites up and down the country, encouraging the owners to avail themselves of our products. In the times between Trade shows and Caravan sites, I was used as a holiday relief for 'travellers', as they took their annual vacations. As I visited the buyers for those various retail outlets, I took the opportunity to speak of the Gospel of our Lord Jesus Christ and the Church (a page out of Georges book).

It was interesting to find that some of the buyers would quickly place their orders and then call the available staff together and say to me, "Tell us more about Jesus and about the Church." I share that because I think that sometimes we get the idea that people in the work places in our cities are not interested in the Gospel News, but the problem is more likely to be that we don't talk about it when the opportunity is given to us.

The opportunities that were opening to me led to me having a greater desire to share that Gospel News. There were times when the Women's Guild or some other group would have speakers unable to turn up on a given date. I would be called in to be the speaker for the day. With my time being flexible, I was able to come off my 'journey' and fill in as guest speaker.

The Move

With a baby on board, no bathroom facilities, a shared 'cludge' on the stairs, and a shared wash house, it was not ideal. With a regular job and a more settled style of life, we began thinking about buying a house. With budget in hand and a deep sense of trepidation I went to see the local bank manager. He very graciously listened to my plea for a loan towards a deposit for a mortgage and I was encouraged that he asked quite a bit about my Church involvement.

Then came the crunch, when he asked what sum I had in mind and I said, "Could you give me three hundred pounds?" For a few moments, which to me seemed an age, he kept looking at the notes he had been making, then looking at me.

Eventually he said, "No". After a pause he said again, "No, the bank won't lend you three hundred pounds, but on my authority, it will lend you four hundred pounds." He went on to explain that he thought that I had trimmed my budget too finely and that I would need the extra one hundred pounds.

I give thanks to God for the wisdom and understanding shown by that Bank manager, as it turned out that he was right. Though I did not appreciate it at the time, I now know that God was fashioning the way for our future. The house of our dreams became available at the price we could afford. It was in a lovely residential area in Garrowhill; a semi-detached bungalow with garage out back and out front a garden, convenient for bus and rail travel to the city. It was a lovely time for us, lovely neighbours, friends for the girls, George and Betty just down the road, our own door

I was finding the Readers course interesting and challenging, but I wasn't sure if it was for me; however I persevered with it. At some stage I was sharing my thoughts with one of the leaders, and I think he detected my uncertainty regarding becoming a Reader. He mentioned the position of Missionary within the Church of Scotland. I recall that the mention of the word Missionary caused a strange stirring in my spirit, that led me to enquire regarding what was involved in becoming a Missionary within the Church of Scotland. I got myself an application form for St. Colm's Missionary College, Edinburgh, which at that time was the residential training centre for Missionaries for the Church of Scotland. There I was faced with the question regarding Educational Qualifications and had to answer, *'None'*. I just wish that there had been a question like; *'Zeal for the Lord'?* Where I could have answered, *'Major'*. However, with a prayer of hope rather than expectation, I sent it off.

It was about that time that the absurdity of it all, the reality of it set in. Here I was, with a wife and family of two girls, with a mortgage, with a job which paid good money and included a company car, and was thinking of giving up all that, leaving my family life and going away to Edinburgh to attend a residential course for I didn't know how long. Also, I didn't know what financial help, if any I would be entitled to. Is that faith or folly?

Regarding my work, I was feeling quite guilty about the time that I spent doing things for the Church, when I should have been working. So, one day I went to the boss and shared those thoughts with him, concluding that it would be better for him and the company if I resigned. His reply was that he and the company were more than pleased with my work, my returns, and my loyalty. Whilst I was pleased and encouraged by the things that he said, I knew that in my heart that I was being drawn away from secular work and I sensed that it was only a matter of time.

That time came when I received a positive response to my application to train as a Missionary at St. Colm's College, Edinburgh. The conditions were that I commit myself to a two-year course and that I reside at the College during the four terms. During that time, I would along with my Missionary studies, also study for Higher English. I also got a favourable response to an application for a mature student grant. The money was barely enough to meet our budget, but whilst prayerfully considering the rights and wrongs of this direction, Pearl suggested that she try to get a part time job. With Angela not yet of school age, the prospect of work was slim. But it is true that, *"Whilst man makes his plans, God fashions the way"* (Proverbs; Chapter 19; Verse 2). At the given time Pearl got the job of child minding and caring for the home of two working doctors in Glasgow. A job where she could take Angela with her. With all the uncertainties of such a major change of direction our lives were taking, we took these things as a sign that we were finding favour with God, and, as He does, He provided for us on the way.

Edinburgh

It was quite a wrench for me to leave my family and the comforts of home and enter into what at the time seemed like a 'Monastic' style of life. I quickly discovered that communal living was not without its challenges. Apart from the range of ages of the students, both male and female, there were some from overseas, with their varied cultures and backgrounds, and one or two home on furlough from the mission fields, (usually exhausted). Only those who have experienced it can understand the exposure of character and temperament of being in such a community, where you eat, study and work together so closely; especially at times of exams. Reverend Duncan Finlayson was the Principle of the College. Most of us called him 'Father Fin' and I found him a very wise and patient, yet direct- speaking person. Moira McCallum was the teacher of the Old Testament, and for me, she made the God of the Old Testament come alive, leaving me with a love of the Old Testament which has not diminished. The training of the missionary embraced some fine attributes, in that it wasn't just the study of the Word of God, but also the application of it. Much of the latter was gleaned from rubbing shoulders, prayerful shoulders, with those who had been in the Mission fields.

The Chapel

The Chapel in St. Colm's College was for me a special place. Throughout my ministry I often reflected on that amazing stained-glass window depicting the 'good shepherd' with lantern in hand and a lamb at his feet, with the text, *'He calls His own sheep by name and leads them out and they follow him.'*

Most days of the week, the college community would meet in the chapel for a time of worship in which students and guests were invited to give a message. It was a humbling experience to hear testimonies from missionaries who had come back from the field; some telling of the amazing and wonderful spread of the Gospel, others telling of the dangers and the persecutions. I still recall one saintly man standing there with his hands out in front of him, telling us with fresh tears in his eyes, of a time of sore persecution, when he was imprisoned and the only thing that kept him sane was looking at his hands and hearing the Lord say, *"Your name is written on my hands."*

It was indeed a privilege, and an education to meet with some of those missionary men and women, who came to the college for a time of rest and renewal. I recall one man who was so exhausted that for a week he could hardly communicate, but later he told us that he was so exhausted that at times, he could remember nothing except the Father Prayer and found that to be sufficient to sustain him. The St. Colm's experience left me with a lasting interest in and sympathy for the missionary movement of the Church that bears the Name of Christ. The various cultures and traditions of the people who came through the College were at times challenging.

In a moment when they paused in their mockery, I took the opportunity to ask, "What do you want? What would interest you?"

Their reply was, "'Footie' we want to play football."

Well, that was right up my street, though I didn't say it to them, I just said, "Leave it with me."

"Oh aye, and we'll never see you again!" by this time some were getting a bit aggressive.

So, the youth worker suggested that I leave, which I did, only to visit Colin in the manse which was next to the Church, to tell him how I had got on. With what he had heard of the youth activities on a Friday night at the chippie, I think that he was glad to see me safe. In my earlier conversation with him, he had said that the Town authorities being aware of the needs of West Pilton, were more than willing to look at ways to help the community. So, I asked if he could arrange with them for the use of a gymnasium and a football trainer, with the prospect of forming a football team. He agreed to look into it and I left it at that.

On Wednesday I met with Colin for our weekly meeting and was amazed to learn that the Gym in a local school had been booked, and a trainer provided, for the following Tuesday evening. I could hardly wait to see those young folk on Friday, to tell them the news.

I was grossly disappointed, because the news seemed to make little difference to their attitude; firstly, they didn't believe it, secondly, they were suspicious, "What's in it for you? Why would you do that for us?" and so on.

Well I couldn't tell them that I was looking to train them for the Jesus team, so I just said, "Well, I will be there." Giving them the venue and the time of the training session, I left.

On my way to the Kirk on Sunday I would see some of them hanging about the streets, but they would not recognise me, lest I caused them embarrassment with their friends, I ignored them. Tuesday came and I was there early to meet the janitor, who was not altogether happy about the arrangement and made it very clear that no one was getting in until the trainer arrived. The boys started gathering and they became agitated as they were not allowed in, starting to say not so nice things about the 'Jannie'. Seven p.m., the arranged time came, and there was no sign of the trainer. The grumblings were becoming louder and more pointed from the lads. Then, to my great relief I saw this man coming down the path towards us. He had the build of a gorilla, which filled the Janitor and myself with a degree of confidence. He quickly got to work, imposing his authority, by challenging each would-be football player with the ball at their feet to try and get past him. On tackling each one he left most of them sprawled on the floor. By the end of the session it was a rather subdued group of lads that left the building.

After some weeks of training, I got them registered as a team in one of the local football leagues, only to find that they were rather hopeless; being beat in most games by double figure scores. Not forgetting my higher plan for being involved with them, I suggested to them that games are won not only through training in the gym but also by planning on the drawing board. They agreed to try that, and I arranged for the use of a room in the Church, where we could meet and discuss tactics. The only night available was the same night on which the Women's Guild had their meeting in another room in the Church. Colin was not too comfortable with the lads meeting on the same night as the Guild's women, but he allowed it. I understood his reservations, because earlier I had heard of women on their way to the Guild being mugged and tormented by young thugs, but we went for it.

It was encouraging to find that on some nights I would see those same youths now holding open the doors for the Guild members to pass through. One night I was asked to speak at the Guild meeting and I had a smile to myself when some of the ladies said, "Mr Rettie, those boys you have next door are very nice boys."

Those boys, a few months ago had been the same boys who had pestered them on their way to their meeting. Sadly, the boardroom tactics did not improve the standard of play and the scores continued to be more like rugby scores. Then one Friday night, they, with great excitement, told me that they had found a brilliant goalkeeper. On asking what his name was they said, "Gordon Banks," (that was the name of the English National team keeper at that time) but despite my claim that it was a hoax, they insisted that it was true and that he was clear for being signed for the game the next day.

Saturday came and true enough, one by the name of Gordon Banks turned up, was signed up to play and he was a brilliant goalkeeper. I had also arranged for Colin, the minister and another minister, from the Church of Scotland's head office and the local Roman Catholic Priest to come and watch this game. Well, I said that the new keeper was brilliant, but he had such a foul mouth. With such a hopeless defence in front of him, he had good cause to express himself. His language was such that to my great embarrassment and that of Colin and his colleagues, the referee sent him off within half an hour. The loss of goals was even greater that day. One thing that I would have to say is that even those disastrous defeats didn't seem to deter their enthusiasm for the game.

To try and improve their performance they insisted on having a proper football strip, top, socks, etc. In order to raise funds to purchase a strip, they suggested holding a disco and claimed that they knew of a band, mates, who would play for nothing, if I could arrange for the Church to be used as the venue. That would be possible because the Old Kirk was a Hall Church which could be used for social occasions, but what of Colin and the Elders who would have to give permission? After a great deal of persuasion on the part of two of the team and myself, with our assurance of proper policing of the gathering, we got the necessary permission.

A week before the arranged date for the Disco, I visited the local Police Office and told them that on the Saturday evening that there would be about two hundred young people gathering for a disco, and I asked if they would send a patrol around at times during the evening, They said that they would. Also, two members of the congregation, a man and a woman, offered to help on the night.

The Disco Band arrived on time and tuned up and they sounded good. I arranged for the male Church member and myself to man the door, with a team member taking turns to be with us to identify any known trouble makers. We were all set and were encouraged by the constant stream of people paying their money and receiving their pass to enter. At one point I became suspicious of three lads hanging about outside, drinking from bottles and taunting people as they passed. When I asked, a team member said that he knew them, and that they were from another estate and that they had caused trouble in the past. I decided, that when they asked, I would not let them in. As expected, they approached the door a few times asking to be allowed in and each time they became more persistent. There was no sign of the promised police patrol, so, leaving strict instructions for them not to be admitted by the door staff, I decided to go to the manse next door and phone the police. The police spokesman claimed that they did not have sufficient officers on duty to meet my request. When I returned to the Church door, I was relieved to see that the would-be trouble makers were not there. But was devastated to learn that the door keepers had been persuaded to allow them entry into the disco.

On stepping into the darkened Church, I was met with utter chaos, someone grabbed me, and said, "There's been a stabbing."

51

The victim, with a friend, was in the gent's toilets. I got to the door leading to the gent's toilet and found the three intruders trying to force their way through the door, to continue their assault. But, by what I believe to be the grace of God, we had as a helper a rather large young woman, and I mean LARGE. She had positioned herself with her back against the inside of that door and no one was going to shift her and get through it. With that assurance I shouted to the band to keep playing, I raced next door to again phone the police and found that they now had the necessary personnel to attend the scene. The police station was quite local, and they arrived in minutes and took over. One of the first things that they did was to switch on the lights, which had been turned off to create an atmosphere enjoyed by the young folk.

To my horror, I saw, printed with aerosol paint, in large black letters across the white wall of the Church, the words, *"Colin is a sh-t."* My first thought was there will be a congregation meeting here tomorrow morning. My second was why take it out on Colin? My third was, this is the end of my journey to be a missionary.

My troubled thoughts were interrupted by that young lass who had barred the door against the intruders who said, "Oh it's not too bad." I didn't know if she meant the injury to the victim, or the offensive words on the wall. She qualified her statement by saying that the lad was not too badly hurt, but was being taken to hospital. Regarding the wall, she knew of a place in Edinburgh where you could at any time of day or night get most things. We had all night to get paint and brushes to paint over the writing. This was before the time of all night stores being open, but thankfully, she knew her way around. We got the paint and set about the work. It took most of the night to apply the amount of coats required, but even then, in the morning one could still see faintly, the offending words. Needless to say, that was the end of the Old Kirk Hall being used for any youth activities in the immediate future. But we continued with the football activities and I believe that became the foundation of what is now known as the West Pilton Community and Sports Centre.

On the spiritual side of my attachment at the Old Kirk. I was part of a team, with Colin as leader, a deaconess, and myself. Colin was a very gracious and encouraging person. After a few months, he introduced a system by which each of us took turns at preaching at the Sunday Services. Then on the Tuesday evening, members of the congregation would be invited to meet with the one who had preached on the previous Sunday, make comments and to ask questions. It was, therefore, important for us to keep clear notes on what we had said from the pulpit. From that I learned something very important about preaching. At one of those meetings, a member commented on how he had been encouraged and challenged by something I had said, he quoted what he had heard.

He must have been confused when I looked at him with no little surprise and said, "But I didn't say that." He insisted that I did say it, so I checked my notes, but couldn't find any record of it and no one else had heard it.

After some interesting conversation within the group we had to conclude that whatever I had said, the man heard what God, through the Holy Spirit, wanted him to hear. That happened about fifty years ago, but I have never forgotten it and I remain open to it in my pulpit work today.

Back at St. Colm's, I found communal living very challenging; studying together, praying together, eating together and having the discipline of daily worship together in the Chapel with students and teachers taking turns. I would have to say that the Chapel at St. Colm's, with those great stain glass windows depicting the Good Shepherd leading His people out, was for me awesome. I think that I found some of the study work hard going, but I was so thankful for the teachers who seemed to make the scriptures live. I learned so much from some of the Missionaries who, at times, would return on furlough from the mission field where they had been what I call working the Word. As I have already mentioned, some of them came in totally exhausted, but always ready to tell how God had honoured their labours for the Kingdom. They were, for me, wonderful witnesses to the obedient servants who would go into all the world, to share the good news of Jesus Christ, to cast out the demons and to heal the sick. I took every opportunity to invite some of them to 'mission' with me at West Pilton. One was a Deaconess from Belfast in Ireland, which at that time of troubles was known as 'Bomb City'. As we walked along the streets with many house windows shuttered or smashed by vandals, much like those in her home area, she was obviously very nervous. At that moment the daily one p.m. gun was fired from Edinburgh Castle. At the sound of it, I saw Hilary throw herself down at the base of the house we were passing. It brought home to me the fact that this was the normal reaction to the sound of gun fire in the place where she ministered. Then there was that Holy Week activity involving Sam. In the midst of all those things I had managed to attend to the required studies and shared duties of the College life. Though there was no further mention of a Higher English qualification, I, after eighteen months, was turned loose to become a Missionary of the Home Board of the Church of Scotland.

Missionary

Though I had not forgotten the words of that shepherd, "Ye'll be a Minister." I concluded that I was not good enough for anything more than a Missionary. I had done the best that I could and that would have to do. I was encouraged to think that to be true, when, by the grace of God I was appointed Missionary to assist Reverend Bob Brown at Garthamlock in Easterhouse, which was about ten minutes from my home.

Now, in those days, Easterhouse was known as quite a rough, tough area of Glasgow, but the experience of my earlier life and at West Pilton helped me to identify with the people and to get alongside them. And I was able to complement Bob's interest in the youth of the area. He already had a football team in place and we both ended up playing alongside the younger ones. We also had some charity games in order to raise money. More than once, I found myself playing for a Church leaders' team against a Rangers/Celtic select; I conveniently forget the scores. Bob didn't stand much on ceremony, but he had a way of getting alongside people and a gift of communicating the Gospel truth in a way that people understood it. I liked that. Despite the 'tab' put on the area and the people, I found, that as I met with and visited them, some fine people with a strong faith; I was encouraged to see God working amongst them through our ministry. There are many stories to bear that truth, but I mention only one.

It was about Christmas or New Year time and we were having our weekly Friday night meeting with the youth, when the door burst open and this woman came in. She was in great distress. We could do nothing else but lock her in a small spare room, expecting that someone would come looking for her. Sure enough, a man, obviously under the influence of drink and bristling with anger, arrived asking for his wife. We indicated that we were busy with the youth and that we could not leave them alone. He looked around a bit and then left, muttering to himself about the Church. After the youth left, we met with the woman and we heard how her husband had come home drunk and started beating her up. She fled to where she thought she would be safe. We arranged for her to go to a 'safe house' which we had contact with, and we took her there.

The next morning Bob and I met to decide what should be done about the situation. We agreed that the husband should be visited and I drew the short straw for that. Arriving at his door, I was met with a torrid of aggressive abuse, as he was coping with his hangover. Eventually, he allowed me into his home, where I was able to assure him that his wife was safe, but was not willing to return to put up with such abuse. His argument was that he was a hard-working man, just like his father and was entitled to have a pint with the lads at the end of the week. I agreed that he might be entitled to have a pint with his mates, but had no right to beat up his wife when he returned home.

His reply was, "It was good enough for my mother, so it should be good enough for her." It is so true that many are caught up in a heredity example and don't know any different. I made it clear that it was not right in the eyes of God or of society, and until there was a change, his wife was not likely to return, then I left, saying that I would keep in touch. I went to see him the next day and I found him much subdued and feeling sorry for himself.

I said I would speak with his wife and let him know her decision. I had kept in touch with the 'safe house' and I arranged to see his wife there on the Monday. After some prayerful discussion she indicated that she was willing to return home. I visited him after he returned from work on the Monday. After assurances that he would not again harm his wife, I went and got her from the 'safe house' and took her home. She had attended Church some Sundays, but now she was a regular in attendance, I visited them regularly as a couple. To my amazement, on Christian Aid Week, which is in the Month of May, who was out delivering C.A. envelopes for the Church? Yes, it was that same man. Praise the Lord for His mysterious ways of working. I don't know what happened beyond that time, as I was then being called to another mission field at Culloden in Inverness.

There was another blessing to our work in the parish. It was that one of the elders was the local postman and he recognised envelopes that were likely to contain bad news. On returning from his deliveries, he would look in to the Church and tell us of the persons receiving such letters. We later in the day, would visit that home, just to say, "Hello."

Yet it was surprising the number of times that we heard the words, "You are an angel to have arrived at this very time." We were able to tell them of God's love and provision. Through his work, that elder exercised a wonderful ministry.

painting them all bright colours for the play areas. Parents became involved in all sorts of community activities, with Teddy Bear Picnics and Gala Days, which were in themselves a highlight. Of course, we had a football team. Many of our activities were supported and publicised by the Highland News, and the Northern Times newspapers.

I recall a headline for one Gala Day which in very big and bold letters said, *'SMITHTON GOES GAY'*, I don't know how that would be taken today. What is more, I learned that my community involvement was not easily accepted or understood by some of the Church leaders, but by the grace of God it seemed to have worked.

Back to the Barn

To understand the spiritual side, you need to know the role of a Missionary in the Church of Scotland. A Missionary was someone who was recruited, trained, equipped and commissioned to serve the Church in various situations; mostly assisting ministers in parishes which were large, remote or difficult. We were allowed to preach, teach and do any of the work of a parish minister, including funerals and chaplaincy work. However, we were not ordained to offer communion or baptism, or marry couples, Chancel work. We could attend Kirk Session meetings, but had no vote in its matters. I was never invited to attend Presbytery meetings, where decisions pertaining to the local Churches were made and dealt with. It required that the Missionary had to have an ordained Minister to supervise his work and to undertake the sacramental duties. The Chancel duties. Because the Barn was a mission station of the East Church in Inverness, my first supervisor was Reverend Donald MacFarlane, who was happy for me to get on with the work as Missionary in charge.

Recognising that most of the people coming into those new houses were strangers to the area, I had prepared a leaflet with the Barn Church heading, giving helpful information, like times of buses, the nearest doctor and some helpful telephone numbers. I had contacts who informed me when people moved into a house. I would go along, introduce myself and give them the leaflet, with an invitation to come and worship at the Barn. I called the project *'putting the gospel in with the furniture.'* It seemed to work, the congregation of twelve to fifteen began to increase and it soon came about that we needed the use of the whole Barn. That required the removal of the old blanket screen, and the appointing of pews, which we got from the then disused Old Petty Church.

Because of the state of the loft floor in that area, it wasn't ideal. When on a windy day the big door was opened, causing the loft floor to be disturbed, someone had to quickly dust from the pews the chaff and the pigeon droppings. I think there was a similar effect when the singing got a bit loud. I would see people regularly putting their hand to their head and I am sure that it wasn't a response to the Spirit. If the shampoo, 'Wash and Go' had been on the market then, we could have made a fortune.

Despite those difficulties and the limited resources of the Barn building, the Church continued to grow. Attendance at the existing Sunday School was increased greatly. A youth group and a Women's Guild was established; also a Boys' Brigade Company, a Girl Guide Company and the new school at Smithton was opened. As chaplain to all of those, it gave the Church the opportunity to be involved with so many young people and their families. Of course, you cannot go out and tell people that you love and care for them and not expect them to come back at you when the road gets rough. With so many people from all different parts of the country, with their various cultures and high expectations, there were some rough times.

Many young couples having their first home, and the prospect of high wages, filled their homes with the best of furniture, mostly availing themselves of the credit facilities available; often to find that when the bills came in that they had overspent their budget, which would lead to tension and trouble in the home. It seemed that these things came to a head in the late hours of the night. We would get a knock at the door by someone seeking help. It seemed to be more so at the time of the full moon. As people got to hear that I had contact with most of the help agencies in the town, these calls for help came more regularly. Unable to understand the importance of Church and community, some of the office bearers began to complain about the time that I spent dealing with those calls for help.

Hearing the following story about rats brought it to a head: One Friday lunchtime, a young mother, with a baby in a pram came knocking on our door. She was obviously in some distress and told me how in the morning she went to check in on her baby in its cot and to her horror found a large rat in the cot. Having just arrived in the area the previous week and occupied the house, she knew no one to whom she could turn for help. But she had received our leaflet of information through her letter box and that is what brought her to our door. I invited her in and got on the phone to the Environmental Department who agreed to send out their rat catcher at two p.m. I advised the woman to go home, saying that we would visit at two p.m. I met with him at her house and the rat catcher made his investigation and found that the house next door was still under construction. Some workmen had left the remains of a lunch box in the kitchen area. Rats from the burn running down the side of the houses had found their way in, to feed on the leftovers. One then found its way over the rafters to the house next door, and into the baby's cot. After the rat catcher did what he had to do to prevent a further infestation, he left. As I continued to speak with the mother, I sensed that there was more to the situation. When I asked if there was anything else troubling her, she, with trembling voice, told me that her husband who was a recovering alcoholic, had started work with one of the building companies. This was his first payday and she was terrified that he might be persuaded to join the work squad in their customary Friday night pint in the pub. In England, where they had come from, he had had contact with Alcoholics Anonymous, but had no contact up here. Establishing that he was expected home about six p.m., I assured her that I would have someone to meet with them at that time. I then got in touch with my contact in the local AA and arranged for John to meet me at the address at six p.m. The husband came home on time and was delighted to have contact with the local AA group.

The critics were a little subdued when, one Sunday, the couple arrived in the Barn. He was originally from the Island, but he had not been at Church for years. His wife was from a Roman Catholic background, but after a short time they were both standing before the congregation accepting Jesus as Lord and Saviour of their lives. Praise the Lord. Also, I got biblical ammunition to combat further criticism, for we find in the first Book of Samuel, (Chapter 9), the story of how Saul went out looking for his father's donkeys and came back with a kingdom. I could say that I went out looking for rats and God's Kingdom was advanced. Hallelujah! … Of course, we quickly learnt that when you work at advancing the Kingdom of God in any area, the enemy rears his head and becomes very active.

The following story tells of the extremes that he goes to. There were two young men, near neighbours to our home, who played in the football team and whose mother regularly attended the Barn Church. The two lads were very deeply into science fiction and took every opportunity to involve me in debates on the subject of terrestrial beings and their activities. Their arguments became more and more extreme, and I was left wondering if they were trying to convince themselves rather than me, but I usually ended the debates with the assurance that if they wanted to speak more, or needed help that I would be there for them. The first alarm bells began to sound when I noticed that the mother stopped coming to Church and was seldom seen out and about. Anytime that I called at the house I was told that she was either resting or away somewhere. Taking a street at a time, I had arranged to do house to house visits in the area.

On the Friday night the small team of volunteers began to assemble in the square outside our house, when one of my daughters, who had been out in the back yard, came running in, saying that someone from an upstairs window in the street was calling for help. I ran to the house indicated by my daughter. I opened the door, where I was met with the most awful smell.

Looking up to the top of the stairs, I saw the bathroom door ajar, an ashen looking face peering out from it and crying, "We are dying and my brother is lying on the floor and I can't open the door." I put my foot on the first step of the stairs and felt it squelch.

On looking down, I saw that the carpet was saturated with blood, which was the cause of the awful smell. There was a doctor as part of the visiting team and I called her. She took one look and ran to my house to phone Raigmore Hospital, which was just minutes away. I went back into the house, edged my way up the stairs and came face to face with one of the young men. I can honestly say that I saw the Devil himself looking out from his eyes. I realised that the door was jammed by his brother's body, and I asked where his mother was. With his eyes he indicated a door. When I opened the door I saw his mother lying on a bed, looking as though she was dead. After what seemed an age, though it was only minutes, the emergency crew arrived and rescued all three.

Through much prayer and the skill of the medical profession, all three recovered. I later learned what had happened. The lads were convinced by voices, that they had heard in their heads, that they had to allow their mother to die. She would be the conveyance to get them to another world. So, they imprisoned her and starved her towards that end. On that night they were told by those voices that if they ended their lives, a spaceship would be arriving, on the square outside their house, to take them to that other world. I often wonder if it was the presence of the visiting team of believers, in the area at that time, that led to their last-minute change of mind.

Despite that happening and other dark and difficult opposing forces, we were encouraged that the Lord was advancing His Kingdom in the area, at quite a pace. Despite the lack of facilities in the Barn, no water, no proper vehicular access, no proper heating and of course, the dusty roof, which was the floor of the loft and home to many pigeons, we were able to have weekly

The second story is of a Sunday when, at the end of the Service, I went to the door of the hall to bid farewell to the worshippers. It was a lovely sunny day and right at the door, a car was parked, and the passenger window was down and an elderly man was sitting in the passenger seat. I realised that he had not been at the Service, but I spoke to him, possibly asking how he was etc. I think he said that he had come with his daughter-in-law, just for the trip. The people started coming out and I had to give them my attention as I saw the car drive off.

Later that afternoon I received a phone call from a man who said, "I don't know what you said to my father today, but I would like to speak with you. Can you come to my house?" After spending some time wracking my mind as to what I may have said to cause offense, I decided to make the visit.

On arriving, the man met me, though I had had no dealings with him, I recognised him. he shook my hand and introduced himself as Eric. He then took me into his office and I heard again those words, "I don't know what you said to my father today as he sat in the car?" then he added, "But he came home and said, imagine that man taking notice of an old man like me and speaking to me. When I die, I want him to take my funeral."

Well, you could have knocked me over with a feather, as they say. After affirming that I would, if possible, conduct his father's funeral, we went through to the lounge, joined his wife and his father and I chatted over a cup of tea. It was a simple, straightforward meeting, but only God knew the significance of it, as we will learn later. A short time after that Eric's father did die and I did conduct his funeral service. After that, I got to know a little more about Eric, his family and their interests. He was a first-class marine engineer, a motor mechanic with an interest in vintage cars and he was skilled in coach building.

All attempts to restart the engine failed. As it was a lovely sunny day, it was decided to row back to Dochfour where the berth was. We were very exposed to the sun which was blazing down.

That night, I was to be guest speaker at an occasion at Smithton School and to the amusement of the audience, I got there looking as red as a lobster. On another occasion Fergus thought that the boat needed to have the underside cleaned of any barnacles etc. It was decided thatwe should do that work on the sands at Avoch on the Black Isle. There we would beach the boat and between tides get at the underside. We negotiated the locks on the loch and we arrived at Avoch harbour, but we thought that the tide was not right for beaching the boat, so we tied it up at the pier and went to the pub for a pie and a pint. On the way, we spoke with an old fisherman who was sitting on the pier and told him what our plans were. We must have stayed in the pub longer than we intended. When we came out and walked towards the pier there was no sign of the boat. As we got to the edge of the pier we saw, to our horror, that the tide had gone completely out and the boat was precariously hanging on the ropes tying it to the pier, with no water under it. If the ropes had snapped, the boat would have fallen some feet and likely broken its back.

On expressing our concern to the old fisherman who was still sitting there, he said, "Aye, if ye had asked I could have told you that the tide drains out from Avoch pier very quickly." It had been planned that Fergus's wife Val would collect us by car later in the day, but now we could do nothing with the boat, except wait for the next suitable tide, which was to be in the middle of the night.

I phoned Pearl asking her to collect us by car, which she reluctantly agreed to do. Reluctant, because she had just passed her driving test and the thought of taking the car on to and across on the ferry, which at that time was the only means of getting across from Inverness to the Black Isle, was scary. She safely negotiated the hazardous task and we were rescued, only to return there in the early hours of the next morning, when we found the boat had safely survived its dry land hanging experience. We beached it and cleaned it there. The boat was, at times used for ministry purposes and one day it was decided to take out in the boat a man who was struggling with alcoholism. As we set off, the weather was calm, but whilst well down Loch Ness a very strong wind suddenly arose and we found ourselves battling fierce waves. Fergus was sitting with the man in the bow of the boat and I was handling the engine throttle and rudder.

Over the howl of the wind and the periodic moaning from the man, I could hear Fergus shouting, "Keep its head to the storm!" But courage deserted me, and I opened the throttle and swung the rudder right over to one side.

I am not sure what happened in the next few minutes, but we seemed to be on top of some great wave, spinning like a top. To our relief the boat landed on a calm patch of water and we were now running with the storm, heading back to Inverness. I quickly learned that it is easier and possibly safer to face the storm, than it is to run before it, but thanks be to God we arrived safely back at the mooring. Sadly, the traumatic experience did not cure the man of his alcoholism, but we were all safe.

Back on Land

Things were moving favourably. I was coping, even enjoying my studies at the college. I was being totally involved in the ministry with Fergus, which involved the building of the new Church at Dalneigh. I wrote to the relevant department of the Church of Scotland, asking that I be considered as a candidate for the Ministry and also to the Faculty of Divinity at Aberdeen University, asking that I be accepted as a student there.

To the Church, I made my case as follows, "For a period of eighteen months I was a residential student at St. Colm's Missionary College. There I studied, the Bible, Christian Doctrine, History of Worship, Christian ethics, Church History, Home mission Studies and Ecumenical Studies. I was involved in group Bible Studies, speech training and practical work through my attachment at The Old Kirk, at West Pilton, Edinburgh. Having qualified as a Missionary of the Home Board, I was appointed to help in the parish of Garthamlock in Easterhouse, Glasgow. Then I was appointed to be Missionary in Charge of establishing a Church in the new Township of Smithton and Culloden, Inverness. The spiritual centre was an old barn at Culloden with the most basic facilities. There I was responsible for preaching the Word of God, doing extensive visitation and forming a Sunday School, which eventually numbered a hundred. I was also involved in finding and encouraging leaders for the Church and various organisations. I was responsible for the instruction and preparation of those coming forward to be communicant members of the Church; also, for instructing parents on the matter of baptism of themselves or their children, and speaking with and preparing couples for marriage in the Christian Church. I exercised

The Caravan

I now had more than one major problem; a) how was I going to tell Pearl what I had done, and b) how was I going to get a fourteen-foot caravan that I couldn't afford? The more I thought about it, I became convinced that I had blown any plan God had for me to become a minister. How wrong I was, as the following will tell you.

On arriving home for that weekend, I was met with the news that Eric's wife Sheila had phoned to tell us that Eric had suffered a heart attack and that she wanted me to visit him in hospital as soon as possible. There were two reasons for doing that right away – one was, it put off my telling Pearl of my seemingly foolish plans regarding a caravan and site arrangements. The second was my concern for Eric. During my short visit to his bedside, we had some general conversation and I had the opportunity to pray for him. During the conversation time, I had mentioned my thoughts about a caravan.

As I was leaving Eric said, "I don't know if you ever noticed when visiting my home but there is a caravan sitting on my back lawn. Every time I mow the grass I have to manhandle it about. Having had this heart attack I won't be able to do that in future. If you want, you can have that caravan." He went on, "You know how my father kept bees. He had some hives down in the Grantown area and would sometimes spend nights down there where at times, it is very cold. So, I got him the caravan and had it specially insulated and kitted out, so that in the coldest nights he would be comfortable, so it would be ideal for you."

Barely believing what I was hearing, I said to him, "What size is the caravan?"

"Yes, you got it right," he said. "Fourteen foot and you can have it right away." Much overwhelmed by Eric's generous offer, I said that I would try and arrange for someone to tow it to Aberdeen. To which he replied, "I have a contractor friend who owes me a favour. I will arrange for him to have one of his lorries tow it to the site."

Within a week it was done. Is it not amazing how God works out His plan for his people? Away back in that day when I spoke to that elderly man at the door of the Smithton Hall, that was part of God's plan to provide for me to attend the required studies for the Ministry, fulfilling that word of prophecy given by that old shepherd, "Aye Jimmy Rettie, one day ye'll be a Minister."

Back home, I first told Pearl what I had done regarding arrangements for a caravan and after listening to words that told me how crazy and irresponsible I was, I told her of the provision made by God. That night there was much thanksgiving to God and rejoicing in His grace and favour.

The University

At the Aberdeen University Faculty of Divinity, I found the lectures so different to those of St. Colm's College and very challenging. It is not easy to describe the difference, as both were centred on the Word of God, but at St. Colm's we were encouraged to accept and to believe the Word of God and in faith, seek ways to apply it in the simplest terms to the situations we found ourselves in and in the lives of others. By contrast, the university approach was to encourage us to question the truth of the Word, in a way that made us more knowledgeable of it, and therefore equipped to be in charge of it and any situation we found ourselves in. I am thankful that I experienced those two disciplines; one, the missionary, teaching me that any situation I was called to, I would immediately begin working myself out of that situation in a way that when, I had gone, I would not be missed, as the work would continue through those whose lives had been touched by God.

The University taught that I would be in charge in any situation I found myself in. Nothing would happen unless the Minister said so. I think the tension of the two was summed up in a word of advice given by one of the senior Professors at our last meeting when he said, "Now gentlemen when you get out there remember to leave something for God to do!"

In order to meet the requirements of the Church, I chose history as the subject for my second Higher, and for that I attended the Aberdeen College of Commerce for a year. Being a mature student, I found the studies very demanding and because I could not afford to buy all the books recommended for the courses, I had to spend long hours in the University Library. Some nights, I missed the last bus which passed the end of the farm road where I had the caravan, and I found myself having to walk the three miles to get home. I am sure that during those night treks, I took the opportunity to moan greatly about the circumstances I found myself in and questioned why God would not care and make better provision for his servant. But I was soon to learn that God did care, and in the most incredible way, was making provision for me.

It happened like this: On one of my weekends at home, I went to visit Eric, who was now home from the hospital and by the number of cars sitting about on his driveway, saw that he was back in business. As we talked, I told him of the struggle I was having coping with the various studies, and of my late-night treks. Two weeks later, I was again home for the weekend and learned that Eric had been on the phone asking that I visit him. So, on Sunday afternoon Pearl and I made the visit to which there didn't seem much purpose. But as we were walking out past the various cars on his driveway, he stopped at a lovely model of a Ford Cortina and asked what I thought of it. I said that I thought it was a lovely car.

He said, "That's what you need in Aberdeen."

To which I replied, "Eric I cannot afford a car, especially one like that."

He said, "I never mentioned the price." Then he went on to say, "This car belonged to someone who owed me a favour (there was always someone owing Eric a favour) and I can let you have it for twenty-five pounds. It is road taxed and there is fuel in it, all you need do is insure it, and my company will cover that till you get it done. So, you can drive it away now. Oh, I know that most weekends you will have to leave it unattended in Aberdeen, when you come home by train for the weekends, so I have fixed it so that no one, without knowing the secret switch, will be able to start it." How right he was, for on two separate weekends someone tried to steal the car. One, whom I later learned had a great interest in cars and was knowledgeable of their working, almost took the engine apart and was so frustrated in not getting it to start, that he threw away the rotor arm from the distributor.

So, apart from my academic teaching, God was teaching me of His wonderful and amazing provision and protection for me. There was another incident at University from which I learned something of the POWER of God working through His Word. One Monday morning, I had returned from Inverness and went to my first lecture, when the secretary called me and relayed a message for me to go immediately to a certain room at the Student Campus.

Despite the sense of urgency, I decided that I needed to attend my lectures as a priority and so put off the visit till lunch time, when I immediately went to the room. There I found it full of students holding bibles crosses and such. Lying on the bed was a young student, whom I recognised from my days at the Barn Church. On asking what was going on I was told that on the Friday evening the student had been watching some fellow students working a Ouija board. The student was not taking part, only watching, but something manifested itself and went into that student. The result was that any time the student tried to sleep, some great weight came upon the student and prevented the student breathing.

On Saturday, some fellow students sent for the University Chaplin, who having spoken with the victim and no doubt praying, said, "It's all in your mind," and left. All through the rest of Saturday, and especially that night, the student got more distressed and on Sunday, the friends again sent for the Chaplain who again said, "It's all in your mind." They then called out a doctor and he arranged for the student's admission to Cornhill Psychiatric Hospital in Aberdeen at two p.m. on Monday.

Sometime on Sunday night, the student, then in a pretty dazed state cried out, "Send for Jim Rettie." Hearing that, I asked all except one to leave the room. At that time, I didn't know the story of how Jesus put out from a room all, except for family and friends, when he performed the miracle of restoring Jairus's daughter back to life (Mark; Chapter 5; Verses 40 to 42). Also, Peter did so when Tabitha was raised from the dead; (Acts; Chapter 9; Verse 40). I had no idea what I should do next, but I knelt at the bedside and quietly called to the Lord for help.

As I did so, I clearly heard a voice in my head saying, "Read Mark 9." I confess that at the time I had no idea what was written there, but I opened my bible and started to read that story of Jesus delivering the boy from the grip of an evil spirit (Verses 19 to 29). As I read the story, the young student began enacting the story, convulsing, just as the boy had in the story. When I read the words of Jesus, *"You deaf and mute spirit I command you to come out of him and never enter him again."* Just like the boy, the student shrieked and convulsed even more, then lay very still, as white as a ghost.

As I continued reading the word, "The boy looked like a corpse". I looked at the one on the bed and I thought, *'Good Lord she's dead!'* But I continued reading the word, which tells us that Jesus took the boy by the hand and lifted him to his feet and he stood up. Well, I took the student's hand. As most of us know when you are getting out of bed you put your feet over the side and get up that way, but the student came up like a board and stood on the bed, set free, with her face shining with the glory of the Lord. Cornhill hospital was contacted to cancel the ambulance, and many of the friends were caught up in various emotions, some rejoicing, others troubled, others were amazed, just as I was.

The fruits from that ministry were at least threefold; some of the friends, who were troubled or amazed, realised that they needed to know more about God and Jesus. At least three Bible study groups were established in different parts of Aberdeen, where students had their accommodation. The second fruit is what happened to the young student; rather than being committed to a psychiatric Hospital, she was able to continue with studies which led to a very successful career and a happy family life. The third refers to myself. I learned of the power of the Word of God to set people free and heal them, though unknown to me at the time, God was showing me the ministry He had planned for me.

On the home front, things were very tight and I came up with the idea of cleaning windows when I was home on vacation, and sometimes at the weekends. People were very sympathetic to what I was about, I soon had all the customers I could cope with. It was an opportunity to speak to people about the Lord.

I remember one time, when I was only half way through cleaning one customer's windows when she said," That's fine, that will do Jim".

She looked surprised when I said, "But will it please my boss?"

She said, "But you're your own boss."

Looking up to the heavens I said, "Oh no, my boss is above, He is ever watching what we are doing and how well we do it." About twenty years later, I met that woman and one of the first things she said was that she never forgot what I said about God watching from above.

There is another story that I wish to include here. It happened when, on the first Christmas vacation, I was out walking our dog, a little girl came running out of one of the paths that linked the houses, she was on her way to the local shop. It was a winter's day and she looked quite poorly dressed in a light dress, with only sandals on her feet.

When she saw me she said, "Hello Mr. Rettie."

I said, "How do you know my name?"

She replied, "You used to come to the school and tell us stories about Jesus."

I said, "What was your favourite story?"

To which she replied, "Jesus in the boat."

I asked, "What do you remember about the story?"

She skipped away, clutching her penny and replied happily, "Jesus saves!"

It reminded me of the privilege of having, as Missionary Chaplain, access to the school to teach children about Jesus. Throughout my time as parish minister, I have been encouraged by that story. To tell of Jesus in the boat (Mark; Chapter 4; Verse 25 to 41) to every new intake of pupils at schools and at meetings where I am speaking.

I often tell that story, hoping that one day some woman will come forward and say, "I was that girl and I know that Jesus saves. Hallelujah."

On higher things; I passed my Higher exam for history, somehow managing to get favourable results in the end of term exams at the faculty. At the end of the three years, I graduated as a Bachelor of Theology. Two of my fellow students seemed to have the gift of prophecy and at the graduation dinner, each student found a card at their table placement. On my one was written 'The world is your mission'. It was many years later before I realised the truth and extent of that prophecy I hope to write about it later under the heading Glory all the way. I now had the academic qualifications required by the Church of Scotland to be

Calling

After a probationary period in the Presbytery of Lanark, I was called to the Presbytery of Sutherland in the North of Scotland, to be Minster of the parish of Melness, Tongue and Skerray. It is a place of outstanding beauty, with Ben Hope and Ben Loyal, the queen of Scottish mountains, the lovely Kyle of Tongue, and the sands at Melness and Coldbackie. From the manse; our home; we could look over the Kyle of Tongue to the historic Varrich Castle with Ben Hope in the background. In the foreground was the lovely St. Andrews Church of Tongue, which my predecessor described as the little white Church in God's acre green. The interior was also lovely and a little unusual. In the centre of the loft area there was what was known as the Laird's box, which at one time had over it a lovely canopy, which is now in a museum in Edinburgh. The Laird's box was not often occupied, except when the Countess of Sutherland and family were, in residence in her house at Tongue. The whole area was idyllic and attracted many visitors. With Churches in Tongue and Melness and a preaching station at Skerray, there was plenty of work to do.

As we have already discovered, the enemy, is always ready to hinder the work of advancing God's Kingdom. In less than a week, I noticed two people, a man and a woman, doing something at the end of the Manse driveway. The woman was dressed in a red scarlet dress and the man looked a bit strange. I watched from my study window and I saw them hurriedly walking down the road towards the village. I went to look at what they had been doing and saw that they had, by using stones and sand made Satanic symbols at the gateway. I ran up the driveway, I got into my car and went down to the village. It only took me minutes, but search as I may I could not find those two. Though the woman's dress made her so conspicuous, anyone I asked about seeing her drew a blank. I went back home and prayerfully dealt with the offending symbols, wondering what it was all about.

I didn't have long to think about it because the next day I had a visit from David, a young man who, just before I arrived as Minister, had given his life to the Lord. His visit was out of concern for my wellbeing, telling me that friends of his, from the Manchester area, had telephoned to say that, at a prayer meeting the night before they were given a message for the new Minister in Tongue, to be on his guard, as the enemy was already active against him. I could fill another book with the stories that would bear the truth of that warning, but I would rather use the pages to tell about the amazing work God did in that parish; that He would have the GLORY.

David

David originally came from the Manchester area, and had travelled to many parts of the world, but he now had a croft and kept sheep. I met him as a young Christian trying to get to grips with the new direction in his life. True to form, the enemy had a go at David and he suffered a break in his marriage. By leaving the house to his estranged wife and daughter he became homeless. At the time I had the caravan and David had parked it in an area near to his sheep, so that he could continue to shepherd them. Later, the Countess allowed him to rent one of the estate cottages, that became a haven of rest for many of the weary and wayfaring people, who periodically arrived in Tongue. Some were escapees from prison or psychiatric institutions, others had just lost their way. David ministered well to them, and he was a great help to me and it must have been mutual, because he went on to become a Minister of the Church of Scotland. Hallelujah, Glory be to God

After a few Sundays preaching the Word, I realised that my preaching was different from what the congregation were used to and one member was heard to say, "We don't want any crusader here." One example tells how it became the talk of the taverns in the area. A Christian couple, Mel and Pauline Cook, came to take over the Ben Loyal Hotel. In the bar on the first Saturday night they made it clear that they would be at Church the next day.

Whereby, one customer said, "You won't much enjoy what that Minister has to say." But they came and the Lord blessed them.

Though they are now retired and living in Lytham St. Anne's, they have remained lifelong friends of mine. They were an example of how God honours Churchgoing; as on Sundays, when they didn't have sufficient staff to stay open, they put a notice on the door of the Hotel saying, *'Gone to Church, back at 1 pm.'* In later years, when many of the other hotels in the north were struggling and some had to close, the Ben Loyal continued to prosper. It was good ammunition for me, because when people asked for my opinion on why so many hotels were struggling, but the Ben Loyal was prospering, I would tell them of Mel and Pauline's commitment to the Lord and His Church. Tongue being such a beautiful place, it attracted many visitors from all over the world and the beauty of God's creation spoke to many of them, just as it says in Psalm 19; like the couple who were passing the Church as we were getting ready for a Service and were drawn to join the congregation. Later they confessed that they were not normally Church goers, but that morning, something drew them to come in and they felt blessed in doing so. There were others who were so attracted to the place that they came and stayed, so we had a great mixture of people in the area.

There was one group, consisting of three families, who came from the Corby area in England. They had been caught up in the charismatic movement in that area. They believed that the Holy Spirit directed them to come to the Tongue area to form a Christian Commune and in obedience, they did so. One Sunday, they arrived in Tongue Church. To understand the effect of that, you need to think of this Highland Church with a congregation of quiet, prayerful, devotional people. Into their midst came these new people, fired up in the Spirit, with shouts of "Hallelujah!" and "Amen!", with holy hands raised high at time of singing. It wasn't difficult to see that, if allowed to continue, it would split the congregation and something needed to be done about it. But what? Was the question. The answer came to me that I should start a Bible study time, and try to bring the two groups to some understanding and acceptance of one another. It is amazing how God blessed that. One thing was that some of the new group had musical talents and with David on board, who played the

my preaching gown spread around me, and the first thing that I saw was the other driver's two big feet.

Then I heard a voice saying, "You may be a minister, but you came around that corner like a bat out of hell. I wouldn't care, but I have just dropped my two sisters off at the Church, and I thought, maybe I should also go in."

Recognising the voice, I replied, "Well John, you don't want to hear my answer to that. At least I missed you."

His reply, "You didn't miss me you have damaged my wing and lights." At that moment my organist, who had been driving more sensibly, came upon the scene.

As my crashed car was now blocking the road, she was unable to proceed. Looking across Melness Bay, I could see the Melness Church and I said to her and the others who had come out from neighbouring houses, "How are we to get over there to conduct the Service?" There were some murmurings about the minister being crazy, but God had it all planned.

At that point the organist's husband who was the local doctor had been called out to a patient, and he was returning home and he came to the other side of the accident. Accepting that it was a God- given opportunity, I suggested that she take her husband's car and he take her car, turn them around and we continue our respective journeys. After advising the onlookers to contact the garage to remove my car, that is what we did. Better late than never.

That afternoon, I had a visit from the police who said, "We are sorry but having visited the scene of the accident and made our measurements, we have no other course but to charge you with reckless driving." Visiting the garage on Monday I was informed that the car was a write-off.

Stating the obvious, I said that I would have to get a replacement, to which the mechanic said, "When you get it, would you take it in to us?"

I said, "Why would I do that?"

With highland wit, he replied, "So we can put wheels on its roof."

The less funny side of the story is that, later I was fined sixty pounds and I had an endorsement put on my licence. Since then, the corner has been known as the Minister's corner. And I am often asked to tell the BAT OUT OF HELL story.

The Power of Prayer

We also began to work with the youth and we formed a youth group. To help in that work, it was decided that we needed an overhead projector (no power point systems at that time) which would cost around ninety pounds. With youthful enthusiasm, the group suggested that we begin a fundraising effort. They would wash cars and do odd jobs to raise the money. I have never been in favour of the 'fundraising' method of raising money for what you need, I prefer to just ask. The first person to ask is God, after all, the scriptures assures us that the cattle on a thousand hills are His (Psalm 50; Verse 10). *If you believe, you will receive whatever you ask for in prayer* (Matthew; Chapter 21; Verse 22).

In those days, ninety pounds was quite a bit of money, but they, believe it or not, agreed to pray for it. For the next few weeks, when we met, the question would be asked, "Any sign of the money yet?"

Then, one week when I was preparing my message for the Sunday, I became convinced that I should tell the congregation of the need and ask for the money to be donated. I think I phrased it something like this, "We need an overhead projector for our work with the youth group and it will cost about ninety pounds. The young folk agreed that we should pray to God for the provision of it and I have been led to ask for it today. There may be someone here who feels led to do so in thanksgiving for some blessing they have received, or in memory of a loved one now departed." When you make an announcement like that, it is interesting to watch the response.

Apart from the quiet intake of breath of some, there are others who give looks that tell that they think that the Minister has truly lost the place. But as I looked over the faces of those gathered in Tongue Church that day, I saw a startled look come over someone's face. Someone who I had not seen in Church before. As our eyes met, I knew that God had answered our Prayer.

So much so that when I went on to the Service at Melness Church, I made the same announcement, but I added, "I believe that we already have the answer." Back home, as I sat at the table for lunch, Pearl slid something across the table and I said, "I know what that is, it is the money for the projector." That is what it was, a cheque for the whole ninety pounds – Glory to God.

At the evening Service, I learned who the woman was and on the Monday, I phoned to thank her. She invited me to visit her with the words, "I must speak to you." Intrigued, I made the visit and I heard her amazing story.

She said that before her husband had died eighteen months earlier, they had regularly attended the Church, but I would have noticed that she had never been there since I arrived. But on Sunday morning she awoke with the thought of going to Church. She rejected the thought and turned over in bed, but the direction became so strong that she found herself getting up and getting ready to go to Church. It was so much not part of her normal Sunday routine and she could not understand it, until she heard me make the appeal. Since her husband had died, she felt that in thanksgiving for his life and his love, that she should do so, to have something to mark his having been there. The Projector seemed the very thing.

Of course she asked the usual question when such things happen, "What was that all about?"

I was able to tell her that I believed it was the work of the Holy Spirit, but could hardly believe that He would kick someone out of bed, in order to get them to where God wanted them to be at a given time. Glory be to God. God's grace was extended beyond that, because on hearing what had happened with his mother, her son and her daughter-in-law, who stayed in the south of England, decided that they too should get back into the Church, and that they should have their children baptised, and they came all the way up to Tongue to have it done.

The Organs

The story begins with a letter I received, from a Julie Mackie in North Carolina in the USA, telling me that the year before my coming to Tongue, she and her husband Martin had been married in St. Andrew's Church, Tongue. After six months of being married, Martin died. Julia, being a member of Clan Mackay in America, planned to be part of a group to visit the land of their ancestors. The area was and still is known as Mackay country. Her purpose of writing to me, was to ask if I could arrange for her to have the room that she and Martin had shared in the Tongue Hotel, at the time of their wedding, as the room overlooked the Church. Because of the size of the group of MacKays due to arrive, every room in the hotel was booked. No amount of persuading would make the owner make the adjustment. I wrote back, giving her that information, but added that from our home one could see the Church and she would be welcome to stay with us, for the time of her visit. She duly arrived and we met with a very broken and emotional woman. As part of the group's programme, they were at the Sunday Service in St. Andrews Church, Tongue, which to them was the Mackay Church. I cannot recall the subject of my message on that Sunday, possibly the twenty third Psalm, but whatever it was, it spoke powerfully to Julia and she left there with a new purpose in her life. We had cause to give glory to God. That opened a door for Pearl and I to make various visits to America and to share the Gospel in Winston Salem (North Carolina) Grandfather Mountain Highland Games, Florida, Atlanta, Charleston and even over in Texas. But let us get back to the 'organ' story.

I again had a letter from Julia, indicating that she was planning another visit to Scotland and could she spend some time with us.

In the letter she informed me that as a result of Martin's death, a memorial fund had been opened and as he had such a love of St. Andrew's Church, Tongue, she would like some of the fund to be donated there. Was there anything that the Church required? Now the organs, in both Tongue and Melness Churches, were operated by pedal power to a bellows, and the Tongue one was getting a bit wheezy and temperamental in its performance and we were looking towards getting an electrically operated one to replace it. It was also the time when Churches, for health reasons were changing from the common cup to using individual vessels for the communion wine. We were also looking to do that. The organ, I think was to cost in the region of one thousand two hundred pounds and the Communion vessels about seventy pounds, so I informed Julie of that. To our amazement, the reply came saying that she would be pleased to pay for the organ from the Martin Fund and give the Communion vessels as a personal gift. We should go ahead and get them. Glory be to God.

We arranged the purchase and delivery of both to coincide with the time of Julia's visit, so that she could make a personal presentation of both, which she did. Praise the Lord. Two or three years later, the organ in the Melness Church began losing its 'puff'. We were again in contact with the Organ Studios in Edinburgh, whose representative came and assessed the acoustics and advised on a suitable model. Faced with the cost, it was suggested and encouraged by the Women's Guild members that we begin a fund to raise the money. Pearl was at the time president of the Guild.

One Thursday when she was getting ready to go and lead their monthly meeting I said to her, "Whatever you do, steer them away from the idea of starting an organ fund. Tell them I will be asking for one to be donated." Somehow, she managed it.

That Sunday, at Melness Church, I made the appeal, much like I did for the projector. From the small congregation, the gasps were more pronounced and the looks more telling. On Monday morning, I got a telephone call from one of the elders who was present in the Church and had heard what I said. He asked if I would visit him and his wife, as there was something that they wanted to talk to me about. I made the visit and they reminded me that their son who was interested and active in mountaineering and skiing, had been killed two years earlier by an avalanche on a mountain. Since then, they had been thinking of some way that they could express their thanks to God for his life and mark his memory. When I made the appeal in Church, the two came together and with deep humility, said that they wished their gift to be anonymous.

When I announced it the next Sunday, there were even louder gasps and much praise and glory given to God. When ordering the organ, I spoke with the owner of the Organ Studios and told him the story. He indicated that he would like to be present for the Service of dedication of the organ. I later got a letter of encouragement from him, saying that the experience in supplying the two organs gave him a new understanding of the power of prayer.

Sunday School

With the collapse of the 'commune' project, the ones who had been teaching Sunday School had to get other jobs, which prevented them from attending morning Services and it was proving difficult to get replacements. That, along with the need to extend the youth group activities, led us to consider having a midweek meeting for the young people. We were fortunate enough to get the use of the old school, and the school house at Melness, for a minimal rent. We got a few willing helpers and we kitted the house out with snooker and table tennis tables and other games equipment. We used the hall for the more active games. Part of the menu was, at the beginning of the evening activities, we would share a story from the Bible, and at the end of the games time we would have a time of prayer. For the children's summer holiday activity, we invited Scripture Union to send a Summer Mission team to help us. The team, led by husband and wife, Archie and Morag, arrived and became so involved that they returned for a few years. The young folk loved them. The average day would begin with songs of praise and Bible stories, followed by some Christian activity. Then meals on wheels would arrive; meals prepared by volunteers. The afternoons were mainly taken up with games, excursions, to Varrich Castle at Tongue, or to the beach at Melness, or visiting the swimming pool at Bettyhill, or the highlight which was sailing over to Rabbit Island off the shore of Melness.

I realise that many of the young folk were there just for the games, but at least they were hearing the gospel and you couldn't get access to the games if you were, without good reason, not at the devotion times. I know it had an effect on one lad; we called him little Hugh, who was part of a not so well-off family. One night, I collected him to go to the School House and we were sitting in the car outside the house of a leader, whom I was also collecting. I noticed that little Hugh was unusually quiet, and I asked him if he was all right.

He said, "I was just thinking, when you die, I want to be the Minister at Tongue."

One of the regrets I have is that I did not follow up with Hugh to encourage him in his dream or vision. In hope I keep my eye on the list of those coming into the Ministry. One blessing that did come from all of that is that Archie and Morag, who came from Dundee, remained good friends of mine and later became involved with me at another level of Ministry which gave glory to God.

The Offense of the Cross

It is so true that when we preach the truth of the Cross of Christ many people take offense and the following story is of one such case.

There was a group in the area who were into teaching and involvement of what is termed 'New Age' stuff. One year during what is known as Holy Week (the week leading up to Easter), I was led to have a big wooden Cross, made and set up in a prominent place so that anyone in, or passing through Tongue would see it. One day that week, I got a phone call, from a member of the congregation, telling me that they had received, through their letter box, a leaflet with words decrying Christ and the Cross, and supporting the actions of Judas. I later learned that every household in the area had received a copy of the leaflet. I knew who was behind it and I went to see him I asked him to renounce what he had written and circulate an apology to all, warning him of what the Bible says about those who oppose God and His ways, as recorded at the end of Chapter two, through to Chapter three of the Prophet Malachi, but he refused. He claimed that the Cross appointed in the village was an offence to most people. I had many other telephone calls, from members of the congregations, telling me how the leaflet offended them and that I needed to do something about it.

I decided to weave into my message for Sunday, a greater assurance of the truth, that it was upon the Cross that Jesus died for our sins. Through His mighty power, God raised Him up to give all believers the hope of eternal life. The Cross that we appointed was to remind people of that truth. I am convinced that the enemy was aware of my thinking and was ready to strike another blow. I say that as, on the Saturday or Sunday morning, I can't remember which, I got a call to tell me that during the night, the Cross had been hacked down. That caused such a troubled spirit to be in the Church congregations that Sunday, that I decided what I had to do.

Using the tactics of the enemy, I prepared a two A4-page leaflet containing the truth about Jesus and the Cross and the work of the Church in the midst. It was distributed to every home in the area and I had no lack of people ready to make the distribution. The response was so favourable, that I decided to make that a monthly communication under the title THE STEM, representing the areas covered – Skerray, Tongue, Erribol, Melness. People who would not think of coming to Church, except for 'hatches, matches and despatches, often said how they looked forward to receiving the STEM, which had now become a four-page leaflet, including a Christian message. Glory be to God who gives the victory.

Fishy Story

This starts with a phone call from Mel at the Ben Loyal Hotel, who told me that someone from the programme 'Screaming Reels' was to be in the area and did he know of anyone, who would be willing to join them in fishing for Sea Trout in the Kyle of Tongue.

He said, "I gave them your name and you can expect a call from someone named Nicky."

Since coming to Tongue I had taken up fishing, spinning on the Kyle of Tongue and Fly Fishing on the lochs. I was never all that good at it, but I did have some very good 'fry ups'. So, my first thought was that there must be someone more suitable for such a venture. I duly got the call from Nicky and as we discussed his plan, learning that he travelled all over the world in order to make the programmes. I was led to think that it might be an opportunity to share the Gospel with them. With that in mind, I agreed to take part if he and his team would spend some time with me in the Church, before going out on to the Kyle, and he agreed.

The appointed day came and Nicky, his camera crew and his helpers met me in the Church. One of the questions asked was, how as a Minister could I be comfortable with the catching and the killing of fish? I told him that Jesus was comfortable with it, even encouraged it and I read with them the story from John's Gospel (Chapter 21; Verse 4ff) where we read, *"Early in the morning, the Risen Lord Jesus stood on the shore and called to His disciples, 'have you caught any fish?' 'No they answered. He said, 'Throw your net on the right side of the boat and you will find some.' When they did, they were unable to haul the net in because of the large number of fish."*

After some further discussion about my work as a Minister and some camera work, we headed out for the Kyle. I am sure after that Gospel story we did so with great expectations. It was one of those days when no one with any sense should have been on the Kyle. The wind was howling and the rain lashing most of the time. The Kyle of Tongue is tidal and the tide was right for us to get two to three hours fishing, before it became dangerous. Nicky, one of his team members and myself started our fishing with the camera crew in hot pursuit. I was impressed, indeed amazed, how the camera crew dragged their heavy camera equipment over the sand, in the face of such a wind and rain, and were always up ready to zoom in, when there was any sign of a catch. We had spent over two hours casting into the Kyle without even a bite and the tide was beginning to move us off. I suddenly realised that if we didn't get a fish, the programme would not go out and the things that we shared in the Church would not be heard.

In desperation, I shot up one of those arrow prayers, "Lord we need a fish." Two or three casts later, I was able to cry, "FISH ON!" and as I carefully eased the fish towards the little sand area that was left, the camera crew buzzed about and zoomed in.

When I bent down to deal with the fish, I had another cry, "It's a Sea Bass and not a Sea Trout," but well, it was a fish. I am glad that the camera crew had enlarging lens on their cameras, as it was not a very big fish.

Quite disappointed with the fishing part of the day, we began trudging over what sand was left and as we went through a gate, Nicky sat down behind a stone dyke and said, "Let's sit here a moment."

As we sat there, he asked me what I thought of the experience. I found myself telling him that from the experience, I had learned something very important. He asked me what that was and I found myself telling him how, in desperation before the last few casts, I put up the arrow prayer to God for a fish. How God answered that prayer and gave us a fish.

His reply was, "But it wasn't a Sea Trout."

To which I replied, "I should have been more specific and asked for a Sea Trout." I believe that we would have got one and that is what the programme was all about, catching Sea Trout on the Kyle of Tongue.

He pressed on with his questions and one was, "How do you feel about going for something and getting something different?" It gave me the opportunity of speaking to him about Saul, who went out looking for his father's donkeys and came back with a kingdom.

I expressed my appreciation of how he and his crew dealt so graciously with the Church part of the day. As we did not get what we were looking for, I asked him if he thought that the programme would go out, and he said that he would do his best. There was still a Kingdom part to the whole experience.

Pearl and I were invited to the Ben Loyal to have dinner with Nicky and his team. As we were seated at the table, Nicky expressed his appreciation for all who took part in the day's activities. I am sitting there thinking that we usually give thanks to the Lord before we eat, but also arguing with myself that as it is not my shout, that they may not be pleased. But courage won the argument. I got to my feet and I proposed that we give thanks to God for the day and for the meal prepared for us. Nothing was said about it, but two or three weeks late, Mel got a letter from Nicky thanking him for making it such an enjoyable experience, especially with Reverend Rettie giving thanks before we ate our meal, something that we now do every time we sit together for a meal. Glory be to God.

Fisher of Men

Whilst enjoying the opportunities of fishing for trout, I never forgot that I was called to be a fisher of men and women, but I found the response similar to that experienced on the Kyle that day. But, praise God there were one or two. One family came to take over a croft that was part of the glebe land, which belonged to the Church and was rented out. They had come from a 'close brethren Church', but they and their children started attending and becoming involved with us in the then Tongue Church. However, the grandfather was having nothing to do with God or the Church. Near to Christmas, the school children were presenting a Christmas play, to which parents and friends were invited and of course the Minister. There I met the grandfather, I sat alongside him and I heard how he was so proud of his grandchildren and their part in it all. I told him of the Nativity Service we were to have in the Church on Sunday, in which his grandchildren were to be involved. I invited him along, saying that his grandchildren and I would be happy to see him there. I didn't mention that God would also be pleased to see him there, but on Sunday he was there, sitting as far back as possible, as though he was hiding. But you cannot hide from God and that day God touched that man's heart. He became a 'believer' and he became hungry to learn more about God, Jesus and the Holy Spirit. That led him to ask to be baptised. He and the family insisted that it had to be by total immersion, which in those days wasn't the 'norm' for a Highland Minister of the Church of Scotland.

In trying to accommodate them, I was having difficulty in getting the use of the nearest swimming pool, which at that time was eighty miles away at Thurso. About that time, I was at a meeting with some of my fellow Ministers, and telling them of my difficulty.

With us was one who, after completing some missionary work in Africa, had recently joined the Presbytery of Sutherland and he said, "I don't see any problem. At Tongue you are surrounded by water. Why don't you baptise him in the Kyle? In Africa we did that all the time." There were a few 'hmmms' from some others there, but I thought, *'Why not'?*

On speaking with the family about it, they agreed. The obvious place was at the small pier at the boathouse owned by Elizabeth the Countess of Sutherland. When she was in residence, she and her family were very supportive of the Church. She was delightfully enthusiastic about the thought of the pier being used for such a special Christian act. It was decided that we have the baptism on the afternoon of Easter Day, with David assisting me. As we arrived at the appointed place and time we found a small gathering of people. The roadway leading down to the pier was lined with cars, tractors and all sorts of vehicles, from which people were watching.

On the Thursday, in the Tongue News section of the Northern Times News sheet, there was mention of the baptism and someone, obviously a shepherd who used to dip his sheep, had written, "Well, I have been at many a dipping, but have never seen anything like that." There was another, not so happy incident involving water, but it had a spiritual effect on a few young men.

It involved a young lad of eighteen years of age who was visiting his grandparents in the area known as Port Vasco. He had laid some lobster pots along the rocky shore line. On the Thursday, he went to check them, but never returned. An air, sea and land search was launched, searching especially the rocky area, where it was thought he most likely went in. During the next two days, whilst the search went on, I visited the distraught grandparents and parents, who had arrived and the homes of other members of the family. In doing so, I experienced something that troubled my spirit, I found that I was unable to pray with them. Usually when I visited people, even though they were not involved in the Church, I prayed in their homes. Though nothing was said, I am sure some of them were as confused as I was. When Saturday came with no results from the searches, the family accepted that it was unlikely that he would be found alive, but desperately wanted his body to be found. I learned that the rescue team, now reduced to the local Coast Guard and a few volunteers, were to make their last sweep of the area on the Sunday.

Early that morning, I got a strong sense that I should go and meet with the search team, as they prepared to go out. On meeting with them, I read a Psalm and reminded them of the greatness of God. He knows and sees everything in the furthest reaches of the sky and the deepest depths of the sea. He knew where that body lay and for the first time, I was able to pray with them, asking God to direct them and to reveal the body to them. I went on to conduct the Church Services and during the second Service which was at Melness, from the pulpit I could see the sea and I noticed a flare going up.

I said to the congregation, "I believe we have a result." On my way back over to Tongue, I met a Coastguard truck and I spoke with the driver saying, "You have found him then?"

To which he replied, "No, not a thing."

I said, "But I saw a signal flare."

To which he said, "That was just one of our boats having a bit of trouble and signalling for help." After lunch, with the wind out of my sails, I went to conduct the third Service at Skerray.

On my return, I got the good news that the body had been found. Where was it found? The very place where he had been washed in. That left the searchers wondering why, in their earlier searches, in that very area, they had not found him. One asked the question,

"Could it be that it was because, for the first time the Minister prayed for us before we went out and God answered the prayer?" For some time, that was noised about the area and led to some very meaningful discussions about God and the power of prayer.

The thought that I was left with was, if I had been offering prayer at the other times, the Sunday prayer would not have had the same impact. There were so many occasions, when we saw the mysterious working of God touching people's lives through prayer, I will mention only two. The first involved a young man who came to be a chef at the Tongue Hotel, his name was Sean. Sean had a bad impediment in his speech, when speaking he stammered a lot. But when he was praying at our meetings, he was as fluent as any of us, which was a bit of a mystery to him and to ourselves. On one occasion, I had arranged for a youth weekend at the Youth Hostel at Tongue, to which we invited all the youth groups in the Presbytery of Sutherland. I asked Sean to take care of the catering arrangements, which he happily did. Also, to help us, we invited someone from Carberry Tower, residential mission centre for the Church of Scotland in the Lothian area, to come and to lead the weekend. The young woman, who came, was so enthusiastic that she would sit till the early hours of the morning conversing and praying with the leaders, including Sean. During one of the conversations, she told us that they were looking for a chef for the Christmas season and she asked Sean if he would be interested. That led Sean to go to Carberry Tower and with encouragement from the leaders, he went on to study at the Faculty of Divinity at New College in Edinburgh. He is now a Minister in the Church of Scotland. The last time I heard Sean preach, there was no flaw in his speech; Glory be to God.

The second happened when I was making a visit to see a woman from the area, who was in Lawson Memorial Hospital in Golspie. To the best of my knowledge, she had little interest in the things of the Church, but as the parish Minister, I made the visit.

I found her in the hospital bed and as I spoke with her, she suddenly interrupted me in mid-sentence and said, "You know Mr Rettie, I believe that if you laid your hands on me and prayed, that I would be healed."

Now, I faithfully preached the fullness of Scripture and I often spoke of the healing power of our Lord, in passages such as Jesus saying, *"Those who believe in my Name, they will lay hands on the sick and they will get well,"* but I always thought if anyone asked me to do so, I would run a mile; a spiritual mile. But here was this woman, whom I thought had little or no belief, speaking with such conviction that I heard a little voice in my head saying, *'What would Jesus do?'* I had the answer, I had preached it often enough. He would lay hands on the sick. I did so on that woman, prayed for her and I left.

Three days later, I received a phone call from the woman telling me that she was now home, feeling well and she wished to see me. I made the visit and I found her rejoicing in her healing. She asked if I could arrange for a prayer meeting to be held in her home. I had heard through local talk that the house that she lived in had at one time been a local drinking den with a bad reputation. Though she did not speak of that, I had the sense that she was opening the door of her heart and her home to be blessed by the Lord. I was happy to arrange it. With David leading us in song we had a lovely evening of Praise, Prayer and Proclamation of our Lord Jesus Christ. Glory be to God.

not have a catcher with him. I thought, well, there will be no harm in being a catcher and I got up to stand behind the woman. Sure enough, she went down in the Spirit. I was now face to face with the man who had prayed for her, As he looked at me he asked how I was.

I said, "I guess I am one of the tired Ministers."

He said, "Would you like me to pray for you?"

Having confessed your need, it would be difficult to say, "No" even if you wanted to. So I said, "Yes." He looked for a place where there was a suitable space and he started praying over me. The next few moments were wonderful as I lay there under the influence of the Holy Spirit. As I came to myself, I looked up at him still standing there and I said, "Have I been injured?"

He said, "I don't think so, what makes you ask that question?"

I said, "I taste blood in my mouth."

He said, "Well I will just leave you to work that out for yourself."

As I did, I realised that the Holy Spirit was confirming that the blood of Jesus had truly cleansed me of my sins. Glory be to God. It was then I realised that, though I believed the blood of Jesus cleanses us from all our sins, I subconsciously thought that the sins of my past were such that even the blood of Christ could not cleanse me of them. I further realised that for fifteen years, I had faithfully preached and practiced the Word of God and witnessed Him do some amazing things in my ministry, but all the time I sensed that there was something MORE. I didn't know it then, but I do now, that though I had accepted Christ Jesus as my Saviour and Lord, I was still allowing my past to clog up the channel for God's power to be at work in my ministry. One of the things I had brought over from my past was being slow to learn. That was borne out when on the Monday, before returning home to Tongue, I met with the group at the Centre.

Immediately after the study time, a woman came from the other side of the room and she stood before me saying, "You must pray for me."

I said, "I have to get away to travel home, let someone else pray for you."

"No!" she said, "*You* have to pray for me." So I had no option and I stood up to pray for her. As I began praying for her, it seemed as if the room was shaking and people started manifesting the Spirit. It was so powerful, that if I had not sat down, I would have fallen down.

Despite the experiences on the Saturday, I was slow to learn that this was the Ministry God had purposed for me. I had much to ponder and to wonder about as I drove the long miles home, where I had set aside the next two days to spend in the upstairs room at the Old School House at Melness, doing further study on the ministry of healing as revealed in the Bible. Through that time of study, I became aware that throughout the Old Testament, God was active in helping, healing and delivering His people.

Two areas in particular make that very clear – the Book of Psalms and the Books of Kings. In the New Testament, we find that a major part of the ministry of Jesus was HEALING AND DELIVERANCE. That was the instruction He gave to His followers (Matthew; Chapter 10; Verses 5 to 8), *"Go to the lost sheep of Israel. As you go proclaim this message, the Kingdom of heaven has come near. Heal those who are ill, raise the dead, cleanse those who have leprosy, drive out demons. Freely you have received, freely give".* That commission leaves us in no doubt, but that Jesus intended His Church to be a HEALING CHURCH.

Late on the Wednesday afternoon, the downstairs door opened and a voice with a tone of desperation cried, "You must come and see my husband. He is in an awful state." For a number of reasons, that woman was the last person who I expected to hear calling for my help.

But I called down from the upstairs, "Go home and I will be there in half an hour." When I got there, I found the man in a pretty rough condition. I found myself speaking to him with a greater authority than I had experienced before. After getting assurances that he would change his ways, I prayed over him and left to go home.

On the Saturday evening, I was led to go to the man's home to see how he was getting along. It was an awful night of rain. As I drove past this roadside cottage, I saw a woman in her garden frantically waving for me to stop. Because of the awful weather I felt reluctant to stop but I did. Being more fit then, I leapt over the wall of the garden to see what was wrong. Lying on the path was her son, all six foot four of him, his mother was trying to drag him towards the house. She told me that he had been out in the garden shed most of the afternoon. When he did not come in for his tea, she went to look for him, and she found him unconscious in the shed. In desperation to get him into the house, to get warm and his medication, she started dragging him towards the house. She began urging me to take his feet and she would take his shoulders, thus we would carry him into the house. But I realised that owing to his size and his weight, that it would be nigh impossible to do.

I told her to be quiet from her ranting, looked down at the man lying there and I found myself using Jesus's name saying, "In the name of Jesus Christ of Nazareth, open your eyes." His eyes opened and I don't know who was most surprised, the mother or myself, but her squeal of surprise said it all. Then I said, again using his name, "In the Name of Jesus Christ of Nazareth, sit up," and he did. Whilst the mother was zooming in to try and lift him, I put my hand up to stop her and again using his name I said, "In the Name of Jesus Christ of Nazareth, give me your hand," and he raised his hand. I took his hand and again using his name, I said, "In the Name of Jesus, stand up," and he did. Amazed and encouraged, I, again using his name said, "In the Name of Jesus Christ of Nazareth walk with me." Hand in hand, we walked into the house to a blazing peat fire and the necessary medication. I, then left and went on to see the man I had set off to see. I found him recovered and well.

At Church next morning, the congregation were surprised to see the man, his wife and the mother of the young man, all in the Church. Glory be to God. As I pondered these happenings, I began to realise that this was the 'more' that I felt had been missing. I was encouraged and challenged that the mother, who was not too popular in the village, was so impacted by what had happened to her son, that she wanted to learn more about it. I asked around and I found another two people who were interested in learning more about the healing and restoring power of God. To help us learn more about it, I invited a team of three from the Edinburgh group to visit us for a weekend. As part of the weekend, I arranged that on the Friday night we would have an open meeting at Lairg Parish Church, which we advertised as a healing meeting. We were amazed to find that people came from as far away as Caithness. One man, Reverend Jim Challis, even came from Kent in England. Jim became a founder member of, what became the Christian Fellowship of Healing for the Highlands. He came to live in Lairg. Up until he died at the age of ninety-five, he still had zeal for the ministry of healing. Glory be to God.

The response, for people to come forward for healing at that meeting, was incredible and led me to form The Christian Fellowship of Healing for the Highlands. Also, I was given the vision that, in every Church or place where the Word of God is preached, with the power of the Spirit and authority promised by Jesus (Matthew 10), there should be an opportunity for people to receive healing of body, mind or spirit by prayer and the laying on of hands (as Jesus did it). *That vision has never left me.*

Early on the Monday morning after that meeting, I got a phone call from a woman who said that her son had been at the meeting, at Lairg and after what he had heard there, he was insisting that she contact me. I knew of the woman, she lived about forty miles away from me. I knew that she had been wracked with severe pain for some years. On the phone she spent some time telling me how the pain affected her life, how down she felt about it all, and that she was now putting hope in what her son had said about the meeting.

Eventually, I found myself saying to her, "I want you to start reading Mark's Gospel. Every time you come to an incident of healing, I want you to stop and say, 'Lord I believe you did that then, I believe you can do it now, and I want it now', and let me know what happens." I prayed a blessing over her and put the phone down.

Immediately, I was hit with a sense of hopelessness. I began whipping myself with thoughts like, *'What good will that have done her, why didn't you get in your car, drive the eighty-mile round trip, lay hands on her and pray over her, what a hopeless creature you are.'*

Those and similar thoughts were in my mind for the next few days, then on Wednesday, I picked up the phone to hear the woman, with a more joyful tone in her voice, saying, "You won't believe it, but I did as you said and today most of the pain has gone." Glory be to God.

From that I learned three things; one being that healing and deliverance is brought about by the power of God's Word. The second is that distance is no obstacle to the HEALING POWER

OF GOD. The third is a little more personal and it has to do with three days. Going as far back as the student in Aberdeen; I remembered that she had been held by the enemy for three days. More recently, the young man was three days in the water before being found. After three days, that man was renewed, and now, this woman, on the third day, was free from the severe pain that had dogged her life for years. Of course we cannot forget that it was on the third day that God by His mighty power raised Jesus from the tomb. With all of that, I claim to be a 'three-day man'.

From then on, I found that in my Ministry, I was now taking every opportunity to preach and to teach the HEALING POWER OF GOD IN JESUS CHRIST. Quite often advising as I did to that woman – to Read Mark's Gospel and claim His healing. In response to that, people got to hear more about it and started asking for healing. There was one time when I, along with Jim Challis, held a 'Healing' meeting in Tongue Church. Present was a woman in a rather desperate state. Her husband suffered from chronic depression and was not too pleased with God. It had got so bad that, though being a strong Christian woman, she could no longer stand his behaviour and was ready to leave him. It was only after everyone else had left the meeting that she shared her trouble with us.

Jim asked her, "Do you ever lay hands on him and pray over him?"

"Oh no," she said, "that would make him worse towards me."

Jim continued, "He will be on heavy medication, does he ever fall asleep in the chair or go to bed early?"

"Yes, both; he is always falling asleep in the chair and he is always in bed fast asleep before I get there."

"Well," said Jim. "Tonight, when he is asleep, just hold your hand over his head and quietly pray over him."

To which she replied, "What if he wakes up?"

Jim said, "Just trust in God and do it and see what happens." We then prayed over her and she left.

The next day I was walking past their house and I heard someone whistling a cheery tune. I looked over and I saw that it was her husband. I said, "How are you this morning?"

To which he said, "Jim, I don't know what happened to me last night, but this morning I feel great."

I had a little smile to myself as I thought, *'Oh man I know what happened.'* Glory be to God. And the next Sunday he was in Church with his wife. How great is our God?

As I was given the opportunity to preach in different Churches, I came to realise that most Church leaders have lost, or just avoid offering the ministry of healing, in the way that Jesus commissioned us to offer it. Even today I still regret that for fifteen years, I was one of them. For those fifteen years, I faithfully preached on passages such as Matthew (Chapter 4; Verse 23ff) telling us that wherever Jesus went, he preached the Kingdom of God and he healed the sick. At the end of Matthew (Chapter 9 and Chapter 10), it tells us of the great need for healing, how Jesus empowers his disciples to be about that Kingdom Work. At verse six, He instructs them as to whom that ministry should be offered to; it is to the lost sheep of Israel and to me, that is the Church of today. And at verse 7 it makes it clear that it is Kingdom work, and involves preaching the Kingdom of heaven, healing the sick, driving out demons and even raising the dead. It is all to be done free of charge.

How could I have spent all those years depriving God's people of such a blessing? The answer is a combination of three main things, a) I was allowing my past to limit me, thinking that I was not good enough to be part of such Kingdom work, b) I was looking to my own authority (encouraged by my university training) rather than the Christ centred authority that He promised, c) I was not allowing God to be big enough.

There may be someone reading this book, who senses there is that 'more' missing in their ministry, and needs to consider these things.

Expectation

When and wherever I am invited to speak to a gathering of people, I always have the expectation that God is going to do some of His Kingdom work. I tell people so. It is interesting to watch people's faces, when as part of my introduction, I say something like, "I believe God is here with us in our meeting and I expect Him to be doing things in our midst. If it were not so I would have stayed away." Some look surprised, others look around them as though there was something that they had missed. I think we fail people if we don't remind them and raise their expectation of the presence of God at such meetings. I am sure it helps them to take their minds and eyes off the speaker and centre on the Saviour.

After all, it is claiming the promise of Jesus as recorded in Matthew (Chapter 18; Verse 20), *"Where two or three come together in my name, there am I with them."* Glory be to God.

Encouraged by what we saw God doing in our meeting at Lairg, I arranged meetings in places like Golspie, Helmsdale, Thurso and Bonar Bridge. At those meetings, we saw many people healed in body mind and spirit. Glory be to God. But more than that, I found that some who were healed or heard about the Healing Power of Jesus, wanted to know more. That led to teaching and to training meetings and God blessed that by bringing around me a small team of believers who became involved in that Kingdom work.

I recall being invited to a Church in Thurso, to hold a day conference on the Healing Ministry and a small team of us responded. During the day we did the teaching, and in the evening, we had an open meeting for people to receive healing. The Holy Spirit was present in power and towards the end of the evening, the hall looked like a battlefield, with people being overpowered by the Spirit, with all sorts of noises coming from people as they were being delivered and healed. Glory be to God.

I recall another occasion, when I was invited to preach in the Church at Bonar Bridge, which was linked with Rosehall. At the end of the Service, at which I had spoken of the Healing power of Jesus, one lady came to me and with a note of desperation said, "I must speak with you."

I didn't have a member of the team with me, and I was already late for the Rosehall Service, so, giving her my card, I asked her to contact me in the week ahead. During the week, I got a call from the woman and arranged for two members of my team and myself to visit with her. We learned that she was a chronic alcoholic and she felt that she was a hopeless human being, but on listening to the Word on Sunday she felt that there was hope that Jesus could or would cure her. Whatever I had spoken of in my message, the Holy Spirit had stirred up a measure of faith and hope, that was to make her more than conqueror over her addiction. We prayed over her and we left, assuring her that we would continue to pray for her.

The next week I received a call to say that she had a relapse and was again drinking, so we again met with her and prayed over her. The next week was the same, but she and we persevered. My next call from her was to tell me that she had enlisted the help of the local doctor, and she was now doing well. Glory be to God.

I found that Kingdom work was not confined to the Church and on some occasions, we were called to people's homes. One such occasion was when a family had moved to a new house from another village, thirty miles away. They contacted one of my elders to say that they were greatly troubled by an unwanted 'presence'

heaven is near. Heal the sick, raise the dead, cleanse those who have leprosy, drive out demons; (Matthew; Chapter 10; Verse 7 to 8) believing that He will be doing something about the problem in His way and in His time.

I recall that at one of our early meetings at Golspie, we met a man who had retired from a high position in the Church of England and had moved into the area. He was suffering from what is known as myalgic encephalomyelitis (ME) also known as chronic fatigue syndrome. It is a condition which prevents one from walking any distance, causing difficulty in getting out of bed and limiting one in so many ways. He confessed that he was sceptical of the Ministry of Divine Healing, but he came forward for Ministry. It was at the early stages of my being involved in the Ministry of Divine Healing, and I was very unsure of myself, especially knowing that this man had spent many years preaching the gospel to many people. But by remembering how I had for years preached the gospel, including the healing work of Jesus yet, for various reasons already given, I never practiced it, I took courage. In the earlier part of the meeting I had preached about the healing power of Jesus and now reminded the man of those truths, especially in Matthew (Chapter 4; Verse 23ff) where it speaks of Jesus healing *every* disease and sickness among the people. Then laying my hands on him, I prayed over him. At the end, I asked him if he had felt anything, or felt any different?

To which he replied, "No", but he thanked me for seeing him and praying over him. There were others who came forward for ministry, some were blessed with help and healing, and being refreshed in their spirit. Glory be to God.

Three days after that meeting, I got a phone call from the retired Church leader, saying that he had just got back from walking on the beach at Embo and the day before he had been climbing one of the local hills. Glory be to God. His wife later became an active member of the 'Ministry' team.

During my continued ministry time at Tongue and Melness, I had opportunity to conduct "healing meetings" at various places around Sutherland and Caithness and I grew in confidence that truly we have a God who heals in miraculous ways; that Jesus intended His Church to be a HEALING Church and the POWER for that is not in us but in HIS WORD.

The Enemy

I learned then and since that when one is ministering at that level, the enemy gets stirred up, and so it was. I mentioned some of it in the section OFFENCE OF THE CROSS, but I mention one that almost ended my ministry.

I was privileged to have access to the local school to teach the truths about Jesus, but some parents and staff found reason to take offense at my teaching. One day I had a visit from a newspaper reporter who was interested in discussing the subject with me. I saw it as an opportunity to share the gospel with him, but he had other ideas. Our discussion resulted in headlines in a Sunday paper, which read in bold print, *'Highland Minister puts fear of God into children.'* At Tongue, we did not get the Sunday papers until Monday, but just as I was leaving to conduct the Services for the day, my daughter phoned, very upset about the article.

The atmosphere in the Churches that morning told me that members of the congregation had also heard the news. Knowing about my favourable work among the children, they were dismayed. That was a bad day and night for us at the manse. On the Monday morning, I felt I could not go on, especially as it was having a very bad effect on Pearl's health. I was in my study seeking guidance from the Lord.

At about ten a.m., the phone rang and a male voice said," I am Bob Cass from UCB (United Christian Broadcasting), based in Cambridge, England and I have just come from our prayer meeting. Some members had read the newspaper article about your ministry. Though we know nothing about you, or your ministry, the Holy Spirit made it clear to more than one of us, that we should contact you immediately and tell you to stand firm. If it be helpful to you, I can arrange to make our airways open to you." To say that I was amazed is an understatement.

I was about to go through and tell Pearl when the phone rang again. Again, it was a male voice who said, "I am speaking from Coventry and have just come from a prayer meeting at which we were told of the newspaper article on your ministry and we brought it before the Lord. There was a clear notice that we should contact you and tell you to stand firm." How amazing is that?

The devotional 'Word for Today' prepared and distributed by U.C.B has since then been part of my daily reading.

Personal

The ministry of Divine healing was now being tested at home, when Pearl was diagnosed to have Parkinson's Disease. I would testify that by prayer and prescription, Pearl was for many years free from the extreme effects of that debilitating disease. Then in 1996, whilst visiting my sister in Aberdeenshire, I suffered a heart attack. I was taken to the Aberdeen Royal Infirmary where I later had a heart transplant operation. I was blessed that it happened about twelve miles, and not one hundred and twelve miles from a major hospital. The other blessing is that through the amazing skill of the surgeon and the healing power of God, I recovered, and one has to look very closely to detect the scar of such an operation. I returned to work for a short time before retiring.

Retirement

For my retirement we were led back to Inverness, within the parish of the Barn Church, Culloden. At that time, the minister and leaders of the Barn Church were exploring the gifts of the Spirit and so I thought that I would fit in nicely with that. I also learned that my friend Colin Anderson, of the West Pilton days was now Minister at St. Stephen's Church in Inverness and had a monthly meeting for healing, so I got involved in that. And from there, the Lord led some likeminded people to come around me and I found myself putting together and teaching on the healing Ministry, which became known as the 'Exploring Course'. Soon I had a team around me. Also, I was being invited to conduct Services in various Churches in Inverness. The main thrust of my messages was the HEALING POWER OF GOD THROUGH JESUS CHRIST. Keeping to the Gospels there was no lack of preaching material, leading me to claim that Jesus intended His Church to be a HEALING CHURCH. I was following my vision, with the conviction that the Ministry of Divine Healing should be made available at every meeting of God's people, where the Word was preached with the power and authority given by Jesus (Matthew; Chapter 10; Verse 1).

Convinced of that, at the beginning of a Service, I usually remind members of the congregation that God is present amongst us and I EXPECT Him to be doing something in our midst. If it was not so, I would have stayed in bed. It was and still is interesting to see the faces and the reaction to that statement; people looking around to see what might be happening. God in His faithfulness did make things happen and that began to cause me many problems. One problem was "time", with the response to the "altar call". It would cause Services to last way over the expected time of an hour.

On one occasion, I learned that energy as well as time was a problem. It was a day when my first Service was at ten a.m., followed by another, four miles away at eleven thirty a.m. At those Services, I gave notice that there was to be a Service at six thirty p.m. when I would be offering the Ministry of Divine Healing. At the end of that Service, I gave the altar call and people started coming forward. It had been arranged that I use the vestry to minister healing prayer. I think that was to avoid the people witnessing the spectacle of some falling to the floor as they rested in the Spirit.

The first person in the queue was a young woman, and it was then that I realised that I had another problem – it would not be right for me to be alone in the vestry with that young woman. But, by the grace of God there was another young woman next to her, and I asked if they knew one another, to which they replied, "We are friends." With an air of relief I asked if they would both come to the vestry, which they did.

When I finished praying over the first one, she seemed overjoyed and was even glowing in her joy. As I was about to ask them to leave, her friend said, "I want some of what she got." so I prayed over her.

As I led them out into the main Church, I was overwhelmed by the number of people who were still waiting for ministry. It was nine thirty p.m. before I got finished, and I was totally exhausted. From that experience I realised that I needed help and I started taking with me to such Services, members of the 'ministry' team. But such was the response to those 'altar calls' that "time" was still a problem. One example was at one Church, where the Church Service started at eleven a.m. and in response to the altar call so many people came forward. Although the rest of the congregation left we, even with the team, were still ministering at two p.m. As I was praying over the last one I noticed from the corner of my eye a movement right at the back of the Church.

As I walked up the aisle to leave, I saw the minister sitting in the back seat. I apologised for being so long, to which he replied, "No need, I am pleased with the response, but my Church Officer phoned me a little while ago and said, 'that man is still here and I need to get my dinner. Would you go down and lock up'." We were beginning to learn that when you allow God to be God in Church Services, time goes out the window.

Knowing that most Churches have a difficulty with that, I would try and have the 'altar calls' at the end of the Service. I would let the people know that if they were not to be involved, they could leave. But one time, I realised that in being open to God's bidding, it does not always work out as we plan or want. There was one occasion when, at the end of my preaching the message I felt led to give an altar call, and I was overwhelmed with the response. It was a Service in which the children came into the congregation at the end and we had not yet got to that point. There was a line two deep and It took ages for me to minister to each person. Being much over the usual time, I later learned that the children were 'frazzled' waiting, but I was impressed that no one seemed to have left the congregation.

On seeing people out, I made comment to that effect to one of the leaders and got the following reply, "Well they wouldn't would they, because you hadn't at that point asked for the offering." Praise God, that Church went on to have a healing ministry offered at the end of every Service.

The Team

In the following chapters I will mention THE MINISTRY TEAM They were the fruits of an exploring course which I prepared, to have people trained in the Ministry of Divine Healing. The Exploring Course allows interested people to explore the mystery and ministry of Divine Healing, centred on how Jesus did it. Locally, it involves five evening meetings. Further afield, we do it on two extended week-ends.

The content of the course is: 1) Gathering in 2) Sending out with authority 3) Gifts of the Spirit 4) The power of prayer 5) Practice and preparation and finally a teaching on the Ministry of Deliverance. I have been privileged to do that course in places like Malawi, South Africa, the Congo, and nearer home Tobermory, Dundee, Forres, Evanton, Alness, Lairg, Portmahomack, Thurso, Lochcarron, and Inverness. As a result, hundreds of Christians have learned that Jesus intended His Church to be a HEALING CHURCH. Some individuals follow on and become members of the Ministry Team, willing and ready to offer prayer for healing as opportunities arise. One of the blessings of our ministries, is that it cuts across the denominational barriers. We have people from most denominations exploring with us and the Ministry team is made up of people from different Churches.

Another blessing is that we don't go into an area and only 'do our stuff', we also equip people to be part of a HEALING CHURCH or Fellowship. This will be so important for that day when God's Spirit will move mightily in all parts of the world, and people will be crying out for God and His salvation and whatever they may think of the Church of today, they will be led there. Sadly, many Churches will not know what is happening and what to do about it, but those who have EXPLORED THE MINISTRY of Divine healing will be able to say, "I know what is happening and will be effective in dealing with it." Glory be to God.

It was in Malawi that I was brought face to face with how the Church lets its people down. I had finished the Exploring Course, and was invited to meet with the Pastors involved. One of them said, and I quote, *"If the early missionaries who came from your Church to our land had been teaching what you have been teaching, we today, would not have the problem we have with witch doctors and such."*

With the increased spiritualist activity going on in our own country, the Church needs to seriously consider that statement. The following story speaks into that. One day, I and a team member were returning from a ministry in the north, when my phone rang. It was the secretary of the chaplaincy of Raigmore Hospital. Her request was that we come immediately to the hospital. We arrived at the hospital to find three young people, two boys and a girl. We learned that the grandmother of one of them had died, and someone suggested that they consult a Ouija board by which they could get in touch with the dead grandmother. On the Friday evening they did that, and some spirit came from the board into them, convincing them that if they went to sleep, they would die and join the grandmother. All that night they got no sleep, even on Saturday they dared not sleep.

On Sunday morning, they, in desperation thought, "We will go to the Church and they will help us."

On arriving at the Church and speaking with the leader, they were told; "We don't know how to deal with this you must go to the hospital."

On Monday, they went to the hospital only to be told that they could not help, and that they would have to go to the psychiatric hospital. But the secretary who knew about our ministry, said, "I know someone who may help," and called me. We took the three young people into a room and ministered to them in the power of the Name of Jesus, at which the demons MUST flee! and they did, praise God.

As we all came out of the room, the secretary was at her door and looking at the three young people said, "What did you do to them?" They were giggling and beaming with relief. Surely that tells us that the Church needs to recover, and exercise the ministry of Divine Healing, with the power promised by Jesus.

We became involved in the Ambassador House monthly meetings at Dornoch, where the Ministry of Healing was offered at every meeting. It was residential and at one time we held an 'Away Weekend' when a good number of the Fellowship met. We had people catering for us and at our last meal at Sunday lunch, one of the caterers came to me and said, "We are amazed at how you folks seem to love one another." I think that is one of the nicest and most encouraging things anyone would want to hear. It is that love that holds us together and makes members available to form teams to go further afield.

Up north we held meetings in Wick, Thurso, Lathern, Dornoch, Portmahomack, Lairg, Alness and Evanton. In most of those places we witnessed people of all ages being delivered and healed, and renewed in the Spirit. Glory be to God. The stories are so many that on their own, they would fill a book. But for encouragement to the reader of this book, I would mention one or two.

At one meeting a woman came forward to ask for prayer for her sister who lived many miles away and was suffering from severe dementia. The woman was prayed over, and later we heard that the next time she phoned her sister, she found her to be in her right mind. So often we have had confirmation that our Lord is into distant healing.

At another meeting, whilst we were singing our opening praise, I, in obedience to the prompting of the Spirit, went out amongst the people and placed my hand on the shoulder of an elderly woman. I never know why, but I often get such promptings. I didn't say anything to the woman and at the end of the song, I went back to the chancel area and went on with the meeting. At the end of my message, I gave the invitation for people to come forward for healing. As I was ministering to someone, I noticed out of the corner of my eye, the elderly woman being ministered to by members of the team.

Later I learned that when she was standing before the team she said, "How did I get here?"

They replied, "Someone helped you up the steps."

Then she said, "Why did that man lay his hand on me?"

They said, "You will have to ask the man."

She went on to say, "For some sixty years, I have attended Church and I have often thought, that there must be something more. When that man laid his hand on me, it was as if a window opened and I realised what was missing all those years." If she knew, she didn't say what that something was, but I later learned that she became an active and encouraging member of that congregation. Glory be to God. She is now in glory with her Lord.

I never know what happens at such times, I just do what I am led to do, and I allow God to work. He certainly works in mysterious ways, as I was reminded of in another meeting. I was asked to conduct Church Services as the minister had become unwell. As part of my team, I had Hazel with me and a friend of hers came along with her to the Service. I later learned that the friend was very sceptical of our type of ministry, but would come along as company for Hazel. She was a district nurse for the area and like many others in that profession she, through having to lift people, had a very sore back. I cannot remember what my message was that day, but it would have been on the healing power of Jesus. In the Gospels there is plenty of material for that subject. However, next day I learned that whilst she sat in the pew and listened, she realised that the pain had gone from her back. Glory be to God.

You know, I get so uplifted when I see the Word of God live, and does it not say in Psalm 107 in verse 20, *"He sent forth his Word and HEALED THEM."* We have only to preach the full message of the Gospel, believing it, and God does the rest.

I was back there the next Sunday and so was the nurse. I asked if she would consider giving testimony to her healing and she agreed. She got up before the whole congregation and said something like this. "Most of you know me as I am your district nurse and you all know how I have, for ages, moaned about a sore back. Well I was sitting in the pew last week and as Mr. Rettie spoke of the healing power of Jesus, the pain left me, and I have had a week free from pain. Furthermore, I confess that I was very sceptical of the healing ministry and only came along to accompany Hazel last week, but now I know it works."

The interesting thing is that, on both Sundays, the minister who was suffering illness was in the congregation, but did not come forward or make any request for prayer. But how blessed are those who live in expectation and respond to the Word. There comes to my mind another situation when I was asked to preach in a Highland Church as they had no minister. As a team, we usually arrive well before the time of the Service so that we can pray in preparation. On this occasion our prayer time was cut short, as the leader of the Sunday School heard that we were in the building and asked if we would follow her to an upper room to meet and pray over the children and the leaders. That was so encouraging. It filled us with expectation that God was going to do something great that day. It was a linked charge, so immediately after the Service I would have to leave for the next Service in the other Church, so I had the team keyed up to attend to any ministry and then join me at the next Church, in time to offer Ministry there.

With so many linked charges, we were getting used to that way of working. I remember that my message was on that Gospel story found in Luke 13, where Jesus meets with the woman whom Satan had held in bondage, causing her to be bent double for years, and how Jesus delivered and healed her. In response to the "altar call", I could see people moving forward as I left. It was later that I learned how God blessed the Church that day with people being helped and healed in various ways.

A few days later, I got the following testimony – "Last Sunday I limped into Church suffering much pain from my recovering broken hip. After your uplifting sermon, I spoke to Hazel and Edith (team members) who prayed for me. After Edith laid her hands on the painful area I was able to walk out of the Church, pain free and straight and the pain has not returned." We read of such miracles in the Bible, but for one to occur in our little Church has left many astonished.

Seven years later, I met the woman and her husband and one of the first things she said was, "The pain has never come back." Glory be to God.

Out West

Owing to retirement and/or demission of ministers, there were some vacant pulpits in places like Lochcarron, Shieldaig, Glenelg, Torridon and around those areas. My name was given as a possible one to help with what is known as pulpit supply.

Being given my name, some of the leaders asked. "Who is Jim Rettie?" and were told that I was a retired minister within the Church of Scotland, which brought the reply, "Oh well, he will be safe enough." Little did they know.

David Scott was minister at Applecross with responsibility for the Church at Lochcarron and knowing my involvement in the Ministry of Divine Healing, invited us to conduct Services in that area. There are many stories of God working His might in those areas and I share some with you here.

One was a happening at Glenelg, which was the second Service I was conducting on that day. At the end I felt completely exhausted. On leaving the pulpit and walking towards the door to say, "Farewell" to members of the congregation, one of my team, Linda, came out from a pew and stopped me and said, "I believe there is someone here who has severe pain at the lower right area of their back" (that is what we know to be a word of knowledge which is a gift that Linda has). But I was so exhausted that I thought rather than announce it, I will just leave it for God to deal with.

I went to walk forward but I was unable to move, I was transfixed. So, I made the announcement and only then was I able to continue walking. As I looked down the line of people coming to shake my hand, I noticed one woman's face and I knew that she was the person.

When she got to me she said, "How did you do that?" I explained that it was nothing to do with me, but was a word of knowledge given by God to Linda.

"If you are that person God wants to speak with you, and if you go down to the chancel area, I will join you there." There were other activities going on in the chancel area, so we took the lady into the vestry. There I started speaking to her about Jesus and His healing power.

For two reasons I do that with most ministries, firstly that it is according to the command of Jesus to preach the Kingdom of God. You don't have to be in a pulpit to do that. Secondly, it helps to raise the expectancy of the person being ministered to.

As I spoke, I noticed a change in her face and I asked what was happening, to which she replied, "I had a warm feeling in my heart when you were speaking to me about Jesus." My mind went immediately to those two who met the Risen Lord Jesus on the road to Emmaus, who when He left them, said, *"Did not our hearts burn within us as He spoke to us?"* (Luke; Chapter 24; Verse 32).

I said to the woman, "I think that the Lord wants you for His kingdom."

"What do you mean by that?" she replied.

I said, "Have you ever given your life to Christ?"

She replied, "No one has ever asked me."

To which I said, "Well I'm asking." We took her through the 'sinners' prayer, which we term the 'foundation prayer'.

As I put my hand on her head calling for the Holy Spirit to seal her commitment, she fell to the floor. For quite a few minutes she lay resting in the Spirit. When we got her to her feet, I asked how she felt?

To which she replied, "Oh, I could never describe how I feel right now."

I said, "What about your back?"

With a twist of her torso she said, "It is gone." I never fail to be amazed at the ways God works to get people into His Kingdom. Praise the Lord.

There was another occasion I would mention. It was when a new minister came to Loch Carron and we were invited to conduct a healing weekend. We arrived on the Friday night for prayerful preparation. On the Saturday morning, the minister and I were standing at the door of the Church, welcoming people to the conference, which was well advertised. As we stood there the minister expressed that he had some pain or discomfort; possibly his shoulder. Without thinking too much about it, I laid my hand on his shoulder and I started praying. The next I knew he was lying across the doorway of the Church. It was interesting to see the expressions on the faces of his congregation, who had to step over their minister as they entered the Church. But many people that weekend were blessed with healing and deliverance.

One I would mention, I have permission to mention the person's name. Her name is Jean and she played the organ for the Church Services despite the fact that she could barely walk because of pain in her legs. At the time of ministry, she received prayer and with a shout of joy declared that she was healed, and to prove it she started walking around the Church, free from pain. Glory be to God.

That afternoon, her two sons from Glasgow were due to visit their mother, Jean. They went to her home expecting to see her there, but were informed by a neighbour that she was at the Church. I still recall the look on their faces as they entered the Church and found their mother almost running to embrace them. There was much family celebration that weekend. At the Service the next day Jean, with a gentle demonstration, gave testimony to her healing. Praise the Lord.

There was another occasion when at the end of the Service, we were on our way to get lunch, when this man stepped into the middle of the road and stopped the car. As I lowered my window, he said, "After what I have heard in the Church today, I want you to come in and pray for my wife." I later learned that the man was a military leader and like the centurion spoken of in Matthew (Chapter 8; Verse 5ff), he recognised authority. We went with him to his home, and we met his wife who was in a poorly state. She had not ventured out of the house for months. We prayed over her and got favourable murmurings, but no visible sign of change. We were about to leave when I noticed the pet dog obviously in some discomfort. On asking about it, I was told that it had been pining for some time.

To their surprise I said, "Okay we will lay hands on it and pray over it." Two weeks later I heard that she and the dog were seen out and about and both looking happy. Glory be to God.

Dundee

Remember Archie and Morag who led summer missions with us? Well though they stayed in Dundee, we kept in touch with them. They spoke to their minister about our healing ministry. The result was that we were invited to do a weekend seminar on Healing at a Congregational Church. On the Friday night, we met for a prayer time with the minister and some of the Church leaders. I remember that we were looking at the words found in Psalm 34, and the Spirit came amongst us and raised a great sense of expectancy as to what the Lord was going to do.

On Saturday morning as we started our praise time, I noticed a woman who seemed to be distressed. I asked members of the team to take her out and to minister to her. After prayer, she was able to attend the teaching sessions during the day and she attended the evening meeting. There she was again at the Sunday morning Service. Each time she came forward for prayer. It was not difficult to discern that there was a battle raging within her, but she would persevere and indicated that she would come to the closing meeting on the Sunday evening. We had started the meeting, but there was no sign of her. My thought was, *'She has lost the battle.'* But just then, the door opened and into the Church came the woman looking radiant. She reminded me of Sue Ellen from the Dallas Programme. Praise God, the Lord had won the battle.

It reminded me that sometimes our ministry is like peeling an onion, removing layer after layer in order to get to the core. I keep in touch with the woman and have some great discussions about how the Lord continues to work in her life. After a few visits when we built up a ministry team, there was established The Tayside Christian Healing Fellowship led by Reverend Alistair Keddie, Congregational Minister.

Midnight Ministry

One night, sometime after midnight, my doorbell rang with some urgency. On opening the door, I found a man, obviously in distress and determined to come in. I took him into the living room where I began speaking to him. Soon after my bell rang again, and in opening the door I found the man's wife, asking if her husband was here. I then got the story that the man in great distress, had got up out of bed and left the house. At one point, he had mentioned my name, hence the wife's enquiry. Whilst speaking with them both, the doorbell rang again and on opening the door, I found a young woman, who said that she was the man's daughter and was alerted regarding the situation. So now I had three anxious people on my hands.

At the time, my daughter Angela was staying with me and was wakened by it all, and came through asking the obvious question; "What is going on?" I am sure that she thought I had decided to have a midnight party. In a way, it was a party, a PRAYER PARTY, with the unseen guest, the Risen Lord Jesus.

After about an hour, during which the man received prayer, they left, with the man enjoying that promise of Jesus recorded in John (Chapter 14; Verse 27), *"Peace I leave with you, my peace I give you. I do not give to you as the world gives. Do not let your hearts be troubled, and do not be afraid."* I often see the man going about the estate. It seems that he never looked back. Glory be to God.

Mission

You may recall the note of prophecy that I received at the graduation meal – *'The world is your mission.'* Also, at the time of my Induction Service at Tongue Church, there were present ministers from South India, Ghana, and Zambia who were at the time part of a nationwide tour in the Faith-share scheme. Little did I know what God's plan was for me in the field of mission.

Malawi

A member of my team by the name of Jean whose husband had died, and as she and her husband had worked in Malawi for many years, wanted to have his ashes buried in Malawi. Learning that two Pastors from Malawi were to be at the General Assembly, we arranged to meet with them and found that one was pleased to arrange a suitable plot in the yard of the Church he ministered in. I was invited to conduct the 'celebration' Service and the internment. We then went up to Livingstonia and spent two days sharing with Bible students. As a result of the visit, I developed a great love for Africa and its people.

India

As part of a team from the Barn Church Culloden, I found myself in India, supporting the Good News Ministries. We were involved in various outreaches to the area. There is one I specially remember.

Our leader had become ill, and I was asked to lead the team to establish a Church in a certain area. We met with some people, in front of a small typical Indian style house, one of whom was to be the Pastor of the new Church. Not seeing much in the shape of a Church, I started speaking about our having a SEEKING GOD, seeking the lost sheep, the lost son, Zacchaeus who had climbed a tree to see Jesus pass by. As I spoke about the lost sheep, one of the team tapped me on the shoulder and as I turned to look, there was a man leading a flock of sheep along the road behind us. As I went on and spoke of Zacchaeus, I got another tap on my shoulder and I turned see the same team member, pointing to a man who was watching from a tree across the road. I was amazed at how God provided such visual aids, which I used to the maximum.

At the end, I asked the future Pastor where his Church was to be. Pointing to a rather shaky looking lean-to against the house, housing a couple of bikes, he said, "There." We were invited to meet housebound people, some in great poverty and painful illnesses. All the time I was thinking of the faith of that young Pastor. Since then, I have learned that there is now a well-established and growing Church. O ye of little faith!

South African Mission Directed by God

Jean, who was with me in Malawi is from South Africa. She now lives in Scotland but has a deep desire to share with her family what the Lord has done in her life. That led to a 'mission' visit, led by myself and supported by Jean. During the preparations, we were led to believe that our plans found favour with God. For example, a most amazing thing happened on the day before we were due to leave for South Africa. I was leading the monthly Healing Service in a Church in Inverness, and I was speaking on John (Chapter 14; Verses 1 to 14). I mentioned that Jean and I were due to leave, to go to South Africa the next day.

As I spoke the words of Jesus, *"I tell you the truth; anyone who has faith in me will do what I have been doing. He will do greater things than these, because I am going to the Father."* I concluded with the question, "What greater thing are you ready to do for the Lord and His Kingdom?" At the end of the Service, these two people asked to see Jean and myself. Taking them aside, they introduced themselves as a mother and daughter whom I had never met, but who had contacted me by phone, requesting prayer for reconciliation and peace for her mother, who was due for an examination with the fear of lung cancer. The mother, with a sense of joyful wonder, told how she had been reconciled with her daughter and on being re-examined by her consultant, was found to be clear of any cancer. She came to the Service, with her daughter to give thanks for the prayers through which she was reconciled to her daughter, and given great peace. Then expressing some degree of embarrassment, she said that when I asked the question regarding greater things for Christ and His Kingdom, she was led to do this and handed me a cheque for one thousand pounds, quickly explaining that it was not payment for what had been done for her, but in provision for our trip to South Africa.

We were overwhelmed and greatly humbled, and later realised that God was preparing and providing for expenses we had not budgeted for. Our God is the most wonderful provider.

The Power of His Presence

Arriving in Durban, we had only a few hours to get settled in. Jean with her brother David in the South of Durban, and I at a timeshare flat (gifted by Jean's cousin and husband) in a beautiful Holiday Resort at Ballito, about forty-four kilometres North of Durban. It would have been difficult to be further apart in the same city. It was rather taxing for me, regarding time and energy; especially driving through Durban every day. In preparation for the mission, I was given the words; 'THE POWER OF HIS PRESENCE', and we were to see that at work in a wonderful way.

On the first three nights, I was invited to speak at a Church in the Phoenix area of Durban. It is an area where there is a strong Indian Community and the local Pastor, is doing a tremendous job, reaching out into that area. At the invitation to come forward for prayer and blessing, the response was overwhelming. Each night, forty to fifty people, young and old, would stand in line, waiting hours to receive blessing. Some were ready to accept the Living Lord into their lives, others to be cut free from past involvement with other gods. Some for physical healing, others for emotional or spiritual healing. Many were seeking to get back into a new relationship with the Lord. There were so many and such a hunger for God's blessing that it was difficult to keep track of it all. Sometimes the floor was covered with people resting in the Spirit. That is a blessed time, when we are content to leave them and their situation in the Lord's healing hands. We would begin a meeting at seven p.m. and found ourselves still ministering at eleven p.m. And I still had my drive to Ballito.

On Sunday we were warmly received at Emmaus Community Church. There, I spoke on the Power of the Presence to heal and on giving the invitation the response was again overwhelming. The Service started at nine a.m. and the last person to be ministered to left at two thirty p.m. Again, we witnessed the power of the Lord at work with people of all ages being refreshed, helped and healed in so many ways. Some were asking if we would visit members of their family who were at home. After a snack in a local Deacon's house, we went to visit Jean's sister Lynette's home for a meal. There we met with other members of the family. Their son Ryan and his new wife. After the meal we spoke to them about Jesus and the power of prayer. Ryan and Olivia were very cast down because they had applied for a Bond (Mortgage) to purchase a flat and were told that they did not qualify for a Bond. After sharing with them the joy and hope we have in Jesus, Ryan seemed to perk up a bit. After a prayer of blessing, we left to go to Jean's other sister Denise and her partner Hendry with whom we had a lovely time of fellowship and prayer.

On Monday, it was arranged that Jean would give her testimony before her family. At about seven p.m., some twenty to thirty people met in David's home to share some lovely eats and listen to the testimony. It became clear that people wanted some of the joy and sense of wellbeing that Jean had received from the Lord. That led to some ministry, including Ryan and his wife who were even more cast down because they had, earlier in the day, received notice confirming that they would NOT be getting the Bond for the purchase of a flat. However, they wanted prayer for some direction and blessing in their lives.

Psalm 147 – He heals the broken hearted – On Tuesday, I took Jean out to Ballito for lunch, hoping to show her around the place. We were just finishing a rather late lunch, when a woman came and spoke with us. It transpired that she was the wife of the manager. On learning of our reason for being in South Africa, she, with a note of hope, spoke of her husband who was recovering from an operation for cancer. There, in the dining room, which had by this time emptied, she accepted our offer of prayer for her husband.

Her parting shot to us was, "If you ever come back to Durban with a team, I am sure that my husband will give you very reasonable rates at the resort." We had not spoken of any team, and I wondered if her words were some sort of prophecy for future work there.

My interest was increased when, on my way to breakfast the next morning, I met her husband Graham and the brief conversation went something like this.

"I believe that you spoke with my wife yesterday" Graham said.

"You must be Graham, and I want you to know that we will be praying for your full recovery." I said.

"That is a wonderful encouragement to me and I thank you. This is my card, and I would like to keep in touch, and if ever you decide to take a team over to here, I will arrange special rates for you," he said. I was encouraged that it was confirmed by himself and I look forward to what the Lord has in store for us in that area.

On Tuesday evening, Jean and I were sitting in the car outside the Emmaus Church, praying and preparing for a prayer meeting at six thirty p.m. Jean was led to look at Psalm 63 with a strong direction from the Holy Spirit that she should share it with her sister Lynnette. She decided there and then to phone her on her Cell phone.

In doing so, she heard her sister, with excitement in her voice, saying, "Ryan tell your aunt Jean, tell her." With that Ryan came on the phone and announced, with a tone of amazement, that he got a letter that morning saying that they would be getting the Bond in order to purchase a flat.

We still don't know how the Lord did that, but give Him all the glory for doing it. Three things flowed from that miraculous happening, a) There was great rejoicing in Ryan's family – Jean's is a very close family and the news of the happening spread quickly and laid a foundation for what was to happen in a later meeting with all of Jean's family. b) In the prayer meeting, Jean gave testimony to what had happened for Ryan and Oliva, which resulted in a response which had us, in the Name of Jesus and the Power of the Holy Spirit ministering till midnight.

On Wednesday, I moved to Durban North, which greatly reduced travelling time. On Wednesday evening, Terrance Bonhomme, who was arranging the programme for us, invited me to speak at a Community Church Meeting. Again, we witnessed the Lord come amongst the people with great power. At one stage the floor was covered with bodies resting in the Spirit, being delivered, helped, healed, refreshed and renewed in the Spirit. One man who came forward seeking to recapture the joy of the Lord in his life, lay prostrate on the floor for about two hours.

The Safari

We had arranged to spend Thursday and Friday at a Game Reserve Park. It turned out to involve five hours driving in extreme heat, to get to Hluhluwe Park. It was worth it. Immediately when we got through the gate, we saw Elephant, Zebra and Buffalo. We went on a night drive, but saw only a White Rhino with its little calf, which in the beam of the searchlight, was quite spectacular. We also came face to face with the raw and harsh nature of the jungle when we came upon a recently killed bushbuck, with a Hyena lurking in the shadows, waiting to scavenge the remains. On Friday, we did our own tour, and we saw Elephant, Giraffe, Zebra, and Buffalo in plenty, and Kudu Nyale, Impala, Wildebeest, Warthogs and Mongoose. We saw a Hippo family in the distance and got very close to some Rhino as they lay in the heat, basking themselves in a big mud pool. We were more troubled by a family of four Rhino coming towards us on the road that we were on. Jean's panic was eased a little when eventually, one of the Game Reserve wagons appeared and ushered the Rhino into the bush. What was more lightsome was meeting a family of Baboons on the roadway. We both agreed we would like to do that again, with Jean making one condition, that her companion would exercise more respect, and greater caution with regard to the bigger animals.

Saturday saw us back in the Service of the Lord at the Riverside Community Church. The building at one time was a notorious drinking den, but was now converted to be used as a Church. The Praise was in full swing, and I mean 'swing' when it was obvious that the greater Spirit was now at work in the place. Amid the sound of the music, one could hear the odd thud on the floor, or the scattering of chairs as the Spirit came upon people and pastors alike. It was like the Lord in His faithfulness, brought all the Mighty POWER OF HIS PRESENCE to bear upon that meeting; like a benediction upon our mission in His Name and for His Glory.

That was confirmed when in response to the Word given by me, we witnessed the most incredible deliverances and healings. We were thankful for the help of the local pastors in the ministries. Owing to the volume of people coming forward for prayer at the meetings it was difficult to determine fully what the Lord was doing for each individual, but there were one or two which were obvious.

One was a woman, on the Saturday night, who stated that she had cancer and indicated that she was suffering pain just under her left breast. I asked Jean to put her hand on the area of pain and we prayed, in the Name of Jesus, that the pain be removed. At the end of the prayer, the woman said that the pain had gone and she felt much better. We didn't know who the woman was and she didn't know who we were, but a few days later we learned that a woman who works beside Jean's sister was telling her of her sister who had cancer. It went something like this: "Last night she was at a Church meeting and there were two people from Scotland there speaking about healing. At the invitation, she went forward for prayer because she was in much pain. The man asked the woman to put her hand on the area giving her pain and he prayed for her. To her amazement the pain went from her. For months she had blood showing in her 'stool', this morning there was no sign of blood. She is due to see her consultant next week, but she knows that she has been healed of her cancer." We can only PRAISE THE LORD, may His Name be glorified in that family.

In between the Church meetings we were visiting members and friends of Jean's family, and everywhere we went, people were seeking after the blessing of the Lord. It all seemed to come to a head on the Sunday, the day of the baptism of Jean's niece, when we had a full day of ministry to the seventy to eighty members of Jean's family, who were gathered for the occasion. There were so many blessings that day, it would take a whole book to record them, but for the encouragement of the reader of this summary, I quote two.

One is about a woman dancer and instructor. Owing to a road accident in January, she suffered an injury, which left her with pain in her left knee. This prevented her from competing and instructing. I spoke to her of Jesus, who is our Healer and offered to pray over her. She accepted, and Jean and I took her into one of the bedrooms. I asked Jean to put her hand on the woman's knee and we prayed over her, that the Lord would take away the pain and set her free to enjoy her vocation. At the end I asked her to stand.

When she did, it was lovely to see the look of amazement on her face as she cried through tears, "It's gone! Where has it gone?" In disbelief, she kept walking about the room, stopping only to hug Jean as though she would never let her go. Where had it gone? Our answer, to Jesus who takes our pain away praise His wonderful Name.

Acts 8:7 and many who had been paralysed or lame were healed.

The other is about Jean's brother-in-law, Peter. Owing to high blood pressure, Peter experienced an Aneurysm (seeping of blood) into the brain, causing a loss of memory, deranged thinking, and loss of confidence, resulting in deep depression. The surgeons were considering his case with a possible operation, which was so delicate and intricate, bordering on being life threatening. Jean and I prayed over Peter in the name of Jesus and experienced the power of the Holy Spirit come upon him. We knew that the Lord had done some great work in Peter. Within a few days, we heard of an improvement in Peter's situation. On the 21st October, his wife phoned to say that Peter was now thinking and speaking clearly and with confidence. He is back at work. *He is healed and does not require an operation.* Praise the Lord. The words from Elsa, "if you and Jean came to South Africa for nothing else, it was to bring healing to my husband Peter and I give thanks to God for it."

There were so many other heavenly blessings poured out as we ministered to Jean's family in the Name of Jesus and the Power of the Holy Spirit, with many being awakened to a new awareness of the Power of Prayer in the Name of Jesus; so much so that Jean's five sisters have arranged to meet on a monthly basis to pray together. We praise God for that. We have since heard that a young man by the name of Gerard, (Jean's nephew), who had at one time attended Bible College, but then back-slid, has, through our ministry returned to the Lord and is offering to lead that study group. God is good.

We reflect with thanksgiving on visits we made to other homes; Isaac's mother-in-law who was immobile and refused to speak, having to be led or sometimes carried to the bathroom and upstairs to bed. I sensed and I said that she was in some sort of bondage; she refused to look at me. She kept looking at Jean and allowed her to take her hand when we prayed for her. At the end, there was no visible difference. Two days later, we heard that she had been taken to hospital and was unlikely to live. We kept praying for her and the next day there was a marked difference. Two days later she was back home at her daughter's home, communicating freely and is now being able to look after herself. Praise the Lord.

Exodus 15:26 for I am the Lord who heals you

Then there was Terry's nephew, Warren; a man of forty-two years of age. He was once a successful businessman, until his marriage broke up. He turned to drink, and then drugs. He got re-married

161

to a young woman who took from him the last of his resources and quickly left him. He was paralysed down the left side, was unable to speak, only making grunting noises, and could move only with great difficulty and pain. Warren, had, at one time, accepted Jesus into his life, but his lifestyle had clouded that experience. I spoke to him about the healing power of Jesus and the hope that we have in Him. It was distressing to see Warren trying to speak in response. We both laid our hands on him and prayed in the Name of Jesus. We saw the Lord begin a work of mighty POWER in Warren. His hand, which was clenched, began to open, he tried to kick with his left leg and with help he stood. We could see by his face that something big was happening in and with him. The words were not very clear, but it seemed that he was trying to sing. The next day, we learned that he was singing Elvis Presley songs, which are his favourite. When in Cape Town, we heard that three days after our ministry to Warren, he was speaking clearly, getting about, making his own breakfast, feeling great, and singing. Since then, we were told that Warren is an Aids victim, which makes what the Lord did for him all the more amazing. Praise His Name.

At the end of two weeks, we moved on to Cape Town, where we visited and enjoyed the Waterfront, Stellenbosch, Gardens, Cape Point, Robben Island (a memorable experience). I visited Table Mountain, and the last of what is known as the Big Six was Stellenbosch Winery. Even whilst acting as tourists we had opportunities, in St. Barnabas Church and Jean in the hairdressers and the folks from whom we let the flats, to speak about the love and healing power of Jesus. All in all, it was a wonderful experience and we thank all who upheld us in prayer. May these reflections be an encouragement to the reader, of what we experienced in witnessing people being refreshed in the Spirit, renewed in their relationship with the Lord, set free and healed in and through the POWER OF HIS PRESENCE. **MAY HIS NAME BE GLORIFIED**. I am sure there is much more, the measure of which we may never know this side of the Kingdom.

Back to Malawi

As a follow up from our first visit to Malawi, we, Jean Aitken and I, on June 2007 were invited back to conduct meetings, teaching on the Ministry of Divine Healing. The meetings were to be at Mzuzu, but on the way we were invited to meet with Pastor Nkhoma at Bandawe. That is where Jean's late husband Andrew was interred. Unknown to us, Pastor Nkhoma had arranged for us to attend the setting up of a head stone, which Jean had organised earlier. We were also invited to look at the large new Church which had been built there. Jean was overwhelmed to learn that they had made the communion table and chairs in memory of Andrew. Then Jean presented Pastor Nkhoma with one thousand dollars to buy seats for the new Church. There followed a time of praise and prayer in thanksgiving. The next day we were invited to visit the old Church at Bandawe where there was to be established an orphanage for children, many of them orphaned as a result of the Aids Virus. There they feed the children twice a week, on Tuesday and Friday. It is also an occasion when the leaders speak to the children about Jesus and his love for them. There were about fifty children there. With gifts received from friends and our own, we decided to give a gift of two hundred dollars. Marie Nkhoma had been searching for a name for the orphanage. Some of the helpers suggested that they call it 'The Marie Nkhoma and Jean Aitken Orphanage'. There was much praise given to the Lord and two children aged about six or seven quoted from memory, long verses from scripture. We returned to our flats, packed and were on our way to Mzuzu. There we met with some of the Evangelism team and got settled in to our accommodation, Jean staying with David Steele and his wife Maggie, while I had a room in the Church. We were surprised to learn that Maggie was from Inverness.

The Seminar

After a seven thirty a.m. breakfast at David and Maggie's home, we arrived at the Church hall at nine a.m. There was a time of worship and prayer, with a local Pastor giving a short message on the curse of the evil one, Satan. I then spoke on how Jesus gathered people around him, to train them for the Kingdom work he had planned for them. It was expected that fifty to sixty would attend the Seminar, but they just kept coming in and we ended up with one hundred and sixty. It was now time for lunch and I wondered how they were going to feed them all, but somehow, they did.

There was one man who looked very sad, so I asked him what was wrong. He told me that he had some sort of growth in his throat and on his tongue and had great difficulty eating or swallowing anything. Jean and I laid hands on his throat area and prayed over him, then told him to go and enjoy his lunch. When he returned to the hall, I didn't have to ask, as his smile said everything; he could eat and enjoy his food. He was a small man and from that time on I referred to him as the 'Wee Man', but he was a big encouragement to all the others. Praise the Lord.

In the afternoon, I spoke on the commission given by Jesus to his followers and the POWER AND AUTHORITY he promised them for the work. There were some very intelligent and challenging question asked. I think I stopped teaching at about three thirty p.m. But we weren't finished because a whole crowd of people came forward for prayer, and we were ministering until six thirty p.m. I don't know when we would have finished, if David had not come looking for us for dinner at his home. It was quite a day, but very rewarding to see so many people so hungry for the Word of God and being blessed for their faithfulness.

The next morning, same routine – breakfast at seven thirty a.m. and in the hall at nine a.m. where we found that many people had been there for some time, praising the Lord. I began teaching on the gifts of the Spirit. As I did so the hall seemed to become even more crowded. After more than two hours teaching it was time for lunch. During lunch, I was introduced to the assistant Principle of the local theological college. He had heard that there was a Church Of Scotland minister here, teaching on the Ministry of Divine Healing and he had to come and see for himself. He immediately gave an invitation for me to return the next year, to teach the students.

In the afternoon, referring to my favourite Old Testament character Elijah, I was speaking on the POWER OF PRAYER. After about three hours, it was decided to bless those who were to continue in the ministry of healing after we left. The response was such that we could not get near some of them. So I decided to do the blessing out of doors. There must have been sixty-odd people there. Thinking that was the end of the day, I was faced with a queue of people seeking prayer for healing. Again, we had to be rescued by David to have a meal with one of the Evangelism Committee.

When we got there, we were introduced to her son who was an alcoholic. After our meal, we spent time speaking with him and praying over him. It was again, quite a day in which we witnessed the Lord bless His people with power. Next day, same routine except, when we got to the hall Jean learned that a programme which we had not seen, had Jean down to lead the devotions (Panic). But after ten minutes of prayerful preparation, she led the people like a trooper. I followed by teaching on the ministry of DELIVERANCE, which was of particular interest to them. Soon I realised that they were victims of poor teaching on the subject. There seemed to be a sense of excitement and hope, as I spoke of the assurance of victory through Jesus, at whose Name the demons must flee. By this time in the Seminar, there were good signs of a ministry team being formed. Some indicated that they wanted to be set free from contact with 'African Doctors', which is a local term for 'witch doctors'. The offer was only for those interested in going on with the ministry, but owing to culture or misunderstanding the language, we were again crowded out, as more than a hundred came forward. Again, the only way to get order was to take them outside.

It was midday and the sun was blazing down. However, I eventually got them to form a circle, which grew bigger by the minute, with each one holding hands with their neighbour. I learned that was the African way of showing fellowship. It was very moving to see. Jean and I stood in the middle of that great circle, from where I read a passage of scripture. I then offered prayer for the Presence and Power of the Holy Spirit to come upon us. To my dismay, Jean, standing beside me, was overcome by the Spirit and fell to the ground. There she lay as I went to lay hands on and give a blessing to each of them. Many were overcome with the Spirit and just lay where they landed. As so often happens, they started singing and to hear African voices raised in song really gets to me.

We finished in time for lunch at three thirty in the afternoon. At one stage I thought that it would be three thirty in the morning before we finished. Was the day finished then? Not at all. We discovered a line of people waiting to see us personally for ministry. Again, it was six thirty when we went for dinner at the house of another Committee member. There we met two pastors who were unable to attend the Seminar, but wanted to hear all about Scotland and the Seminar. We were encouraged by their interest in the Ministry of Divine Healing, and at the discussion time, it was obvious that there was a desire to see this ministry continued in their various prayer houses. Personally, I was amazed at how the grace of God sustained us over those three hectic days of teaching and ministering.

Saturday was to be a quieter day. It began with a visit to the home of one of the elders who had suffered a stroke, causing weakness in one side of his body. After praying over him and taking authority over the weakness, he was able to walk freely, and feel a renewed strength in his body. Before we left, his son who was present, asked if he could speak with us privately. We went into a bedroom with him and there he told us that for some time, he had been suffering much pain in his side, but when we came into the home, it began to lessen. When we were praying over his dad, the pain disappeared completely. He ended up giving his life to Christ. Praise the Lord!. That morning the Lord gave out a double portion.

The Evangelism team had arranged a farewell meal. Before it began, we met with the team for a final briefing and appointing ministering teams for the Church Service on Sunday. At the end of the meal Jean and I were presented with hand stitched and framed tapestries, commemorating our visit to St Andrew's, Church, Mzuzu, in the Synod of Livingstonia.

Sunday, eight a.m. came all too soon. We found ourselves in the Church, which was rapidly filling up as people gathered for worship. By eight thirty a.m., most of the thousand seats were filled and there was a great sense of expectation. The Lord gave me to speak on the "Ministry of the Laying on of hands." I was conscious of the fact that another Service was due to commence at ten thirty a.m. So, at the end I asked for only one person in need of healing to come forward, so that I could demonstrate the simplicity of our Ministry of the laying on of hands. There would be an opportunity for others to meet with us in the hall, after the Service.

One woman from near the front came forward and as I and one my appointed team prepared to minister to her, I noticed another woman from half way up the Church struggling to her feet. Slowly and heavily dependent on her walking aids, she began making her way to the front. No matter how I tried to discourage her from doing so, it was obvious that nothing nor anyone was going to stop her. Then, as if in anticipation of what was to happen, I saw Jean leading her team on to the stage. The first woman was complaining of pains in her chest. As we prayed over her she rested in the Spirit, after which she said that the pain had gone completely. By this time, the second woman had arrived and with the help of Jean's team struggled on to the stage. Jean and her team began praying over her. We watched as they encouraged her to walk alongside the stage unaided, which was obviously difficult for her. So, we watched as they prayed some more over her, at which she rested in the Spirit. On getting to her feet, the woman went striding off the stage, and with arms held high and the words, "I HAVE BEEN HEALED", walked freely back to her husband who was in floods of tears.

The Church erupted in praise and applause as her walking aids were handed to a friend. "Hallelujah!" was the cry. As we moved to the hall, hundreds of people crowded in and it became a milling mass of people, reaching out to be touched. With the newly trained teams, it was difficult to get any order into the situation, made more difficult with many people resting in the Spirit. Jean was overwhelmed at how God was blessing people. For the first time she witnessed children of six or seven being overcome by the Spirit. She had one blessed experience, when a mother brought forward her daughter of seven years of age.

She asked the child what she would like Jesus to do for her, and the child replied, "Give me wisdom" – out of the mouths of babes … At one point I noticed that Jean was missing. No one seemed to know where she went. It was later that I learned one couple insisted that she go and pray for their child who was in the local hospital. With one of the team, she was whisked away in a car. The medical staff had given up hope for the child, but when the parents witnessed what was happening in the hall, their hope was raised. The following testimony, which we got later, speaks for itself.

Quote, "Jean prayed for our son at St. John's hospital in Mzuzu. We thank the Lord so much for blessing you with His love and healing power. Our son was healed, has recovered and is healthy. We had lost all hope, but you restored our faith. Mostly you shared your love and healed our son, Mbonisle. We pray that GOD continues to bless you abundantly and hope more lives get healed and saved. Thank you, we hope one day that we will be able to thank you in person. GOD BLESS YOU."

Back in the hall, the five teams were kept busy ministering till four p.m., when Jean and I were rescued for a late lunch pre-arranged at a local hotel. The lateness of the lunch didn't seem to trouble the hotel folks, but it was a bit of a problem for us. The reason being, as we gathered in the Church, Jean met with an old friend from her days at the Sugar Plantation at Sucoma, who was now an elder at St. Andrew's. He insisted that we join his family for dinner at their home at six thirty p.m. On arriving at their home, we were told that owing to the crowd and the need to prepare a meal, they could not wait for the ministering time, so they asked that we minister to them and their five children. After the meal, we set about that and it resulted in a lovely time of family worship, an old tradition which is still practiced in many homes in Malawi.

We were then off to Durban in South Africa and on arriving we learned that two days earlier the hotel we were due to stay in had been damaged by fire and was not available. Fortunately, Jean's sisters had made other temporary arrangements for us at the Blue Waters Hotel. But the damaged hotel meant that we could not use the Conference Room facilities.

Sunday morning saw us at Horeb Temple to conduct the nine a.m. Service. There was an awesome sense of the presence of the

Holy Spirit in the place. We should not have been surprised, after all, Horeb means the mountain of God; it was the place where God met with Moses and declared it to be Holy ground (Exodus; Chapter 1; Verse 1 to 5). It was the launching pad for God's people to claim the surrounding territory for God's Kingdom (Deuteronomy; Chapter 1; Verse 6). In Durban, Horeb Temple is in the middle of a very deprived area, and its Pastor and leaders are reaching out into that area and its people. As usual many people responded to the invitation for prayer, and many were helped, healed and blessed.

On Wednesday, we were invited to conduct a meeting in an Old Folks Home, where we ended up laying hands on and praying over most of the residents. One woman, who had difficulty walking, was touched by the healing power of God. By the time we left, she was pushing around others who were in wheelchairs. Owing to a shortage of staff, one nurse was called in for the day. When she realised what we were about, she asked for prayer for the pain she had in her back. After we laid hands on her and prayed over her in the Name of Jesus, there was a look of astonishment on her face. With laughter she bent down and touched her toes, free of pain. She and we believed it was a God appointment.

There was also one woman, who owing to her excessive weight was bed-ridden, and unable to move her limbs. At her request, we prayed over her, and to the amazement of the staff, as we left she raised her massive arm to wave us good-bye. The next Sunday, we were invited to the Gabriel Church, which followed the Anglican form of liturgy, but are sufficiently free in the Spirit to vary it for our visit. There, I spoke on the ministry of the LAYING ON OF HANDS. In response to the invitation, a queue quickly formed seeking ministry. We had started a seven a.m. and it was now time for the ten a.m. Service to get going. The Pastor started that Service, whilst we grabbed an egg and bacon sandwich which the staff had prepared.

Back into the sanctuary and I spoke on the healing of the Ten Lepers. So many responded to the invitation that we had to use the hall for ministry. With two teams, it was three p.m. before we got finished. We were overwhelmed at the great hunger that the people had for the touch of God in prayer. A further blessing came from our visit. It was that Jean arranged for the use of the Gabriel Church hall, for the family get-together which involved fifty to sixty people. The meeting took the form of a Service, followed by food and a Ministry time. I spoke on the theme 'OUR SEEKING GOD', based on the Lost Sheep; Coin; and Son (Luke 15). The meeting, which incorporated a wonderful testimony by Rose seemed to touch many hearts. (Remember Rose was healed during our earlier visit). The meeting also heard an amazing testimony from Alsa (Jean's sister) regarding her husband Peter, whom we ministered to in our earlier visit to South Africa. Alsa was testifying to Peter being completely healed. The reason that he could not be with us was that he is now shift manager at his place of work and could not get time off. How great is our God? It was a time of great rejoicing.

Later we learned that many have come back to the Lord, which is the greatest healing of all. My final testimony is about Jean's sister Lynette, who was at most of the family meetings, but kept at arm's length, with some interesting arguments about the spiritual side. One of her problems was that for health reasons, she needed to stop smoking, but she didn't want to stop. However, at our farewell meal at David's home she was persuaded to receive prayer, in the Name of Jesus. Since then, we have learned that Lynette has stopped smoking. Every time she thinks about a cigarette, she gets a feeling of tightness in her chest. Later, Jean learned that Lynette is again attending Church and the cry goes up. HALLELUJAH!

Democratic Republic of Congo Mission Report

In January 2010 I met with the team to pray for guidance for the future, and centred on the prayer of Jabez, part of which gives the cry; 'enlarge my territory'. The next day, when I opened my emails, there was a call from a Bishop in The Democratic Republic of Congo; Matthew Wilondja, to come over and help them. The appeal concluded with the Macedonian call given to the Apostle Paul. Now, I am used to getting invitations from various areas of the world, but there was something in this one that led me to enquire more about it. The result was, I found myself looking for a team, courageous enough, to join me in a mission to the Democratic Republic of Congo (DRC), despite the reports of the DRC having a history of war – rape and rebel activity. I found that by the month of May, Les and Diana Turner and Linda Ramsay and Hazel Gil, having been guided by the Lord, responded and soon it was all in place and we were off.

Linda's word was, "Do not be afraid of the Giants." The first giant to overcome was the great cost of the mission, which was answered in the very generous gifts we received from people learning of our mission; encouraging us to believe it was God's will that we respond to the invitation.

We were blessed by each being allowed forty-six kilograms instead of the usual twenty-three kilograms luggage in the 'hold'. That enabled us to take a lot of medical supplies and other materials, helpful to Matthew's ministry; as well as presents for himself and his family. Arriving at Kigali Airport in Rwanda, we were met by Bishop Matthew and his driver. We and our extensive load of luggage, tied to the roof rack of an eight-seater dormobile, set off on the six-hour road journey to Bukavu in the DRC, which was to be our main base. Most of the road resembled what we would call mountain tracks. Not surprisingly we had a puncture, which delayed us for about an hour. Arriving late, we found that most of the staff from the border and customs check points had gone home, which further delayed us. It took a great deal of persuading by Matthew, for us to be eventually allowed through. As we drove into Bukavu, we were met by the Oasis Church Choir in all their colourful attire, singing a welcome to us and throwing into the open windows of the van, colourful dresses for the women to wear.

Despite having waited for hours, they joyfully led us all the way to our accommodation, which was more basic than we expected, leading us to look for a hotel with more suitable facilities. Finding a hotel and viewing the facilities with comfy beds and shower, we agreed on a rate, and we moved in. After having a meal, it was decided to refresh ourselves, only to find that there was no running water and mostly no electricity. When we inspected the hotel rooms, we should have asked about the buckets of cold water. For two days, the buckets only, were our washing facilities.

As you read on you will encounter names of places like Kitutu, Sange, Kamatuga and others. These are places which would be termed 'out in the sticks', where there is great poverty. In some cases where the Church is reluctant to go, but that is where Bishop Matthew establishes Churches. We have been humbled to be there with Matthew to experience the poverty and the danger but privileged to witness the hunger those people have for the Word of God. As a Fellowship, based on faith, we have endeavoured to support Matthew in that work, and God has graciously blessed us in our endeavours, mainly through donations from those who hear of our work in the Democratic Republic of the Congo.

On the Saturday, in the Swedish Free Mission Church, we met with pastors from various denominations. At the end of my introductory talk, an invitation was given for anyone requiring ministry so that we could demonstrate our form of ministry. One pastor came forward, saying that he had severe pain in his stomach. On receiving prayer and laying on of hands, he was immediately set free. From there, we went to the office of the Bishop of the Swedish Free Mission, who had asked for private prayer. He had been to America for healing but had not felt better and continued to have awful pain in his head. As we prayed over him, Ruth saw a serpent like creature come out of his mouth. He was there and then – 'delivered' in his very office. Reports are that he still keeps well. From there, we went to the office of another Bishop who suffered from depression, and he too was set free. We later visited an orphan school, where Linda and Les gave the children a talk on the Prophet Jonah. From there, we visited a clinic for the sick and found the place and the materials very basic. There, one of the choir members was very sick with malaria. As we prayed over her and some other children, we found all to be healed.

The next morning, we were in Matthew's Church at Bukavu where, after giving a message from the letter to the Romans, an invitation was given for people to receive prayer for healing and renewal. Many people responded and received healing and deliverance. Some of the Pastors responded, asking for more power. In the afternoon, there was a meeting for the women, many of whom were victims of the war. Linda spoke to them on the text from Romans; (Chapter 8), *"Nothing can separate us from God's love in Jesus Christ."* Two of the women were appointed spokespersons and we heard of some of the most atrocious brutality, too awful to write of here.

Our next stop was Kamatuga, (Matthew's home village). It is a gold mining village, where once there was a large slave market. Up to twenty million slaves were taken from the Congo to Tanzania. The journey from Bukavu to Kamatuga took six hours. On the journey, we were on many occasions stopped by village elders who asked for money in order to pass through their village.

But Matthew, wearing his 'dog collar', used God's authority for us to avoid payment. We were welcomed and given hospitality by pastors from many different denominations – Church of God, Lutheran, Baptist, Methodist, Pentecostal, Army etc. Some had travelled great distances to meet and to welcome us.

At the Service next day, I spoke on the healing power of God through the Old and New Testaments, resulting in an amazing outpouring of the Holy Spirit. The pastors who came forward were anointed with power and many gifts of the Spirit. Many women leaders were anointed with oil, causing many of them to rest in the Spirit. At that Service, every man, woman and child was prayed over with the laying on of hands. Even the street children who followed us to Church, were prayed over.

The next morning, we were up at five thirty a.m. After a breakfast of bread and honey, we were off back to Bukavu. On the way we stopped to speak to a man who had caught a large catfish, which Matthew bought and had it tied to the front of the vehicle. We stopped at various villages where Matthew met with some of his extended family. In one village he bought pineapples from a street vender. In another village we loaded on some charcoal. Matthew saw it all as God's provision. There was what I would term, a higher provision involving our driver Bonane. As we passed through one village Bonane saw his father who, having gone off with another woman, had been missing for ten years. At the last Service, I had asked people to hold out their hands that God might give them the desire of their heart. Unknown to any of us, Bonane had asked that his father return to his family. The meeting at that village led to his father returning to his home. We truly have an amazing God.

This leaves us with the challenge found in the Letter of James, *"You have not because you ask not."* At about eleven a.m. our journey was brought to a sudden stop, owing to a road accident, where a low loader truck had shed its load of a High Mack Machine, which belonged to the Chinese. The trailer was hanging over the edge of a gorge, into which the High Mack had fallen. We were told that one of the escort army personal had been killed and another was taken to hospital. It would have been possible to move the cab of the trailer to let traffic through, but the Chinese refused, claiming that it would risk the trailer. The accident happened the day before and many vehicles were now in a queue, with some people having a load of perishables for the market. As we waited, I saw a soldier approaching, and he was obviously drunk, and he carried a Kalashnikov submachine gun.

On seeing the white people, he staggered towards us and pointing the gun at me, he said, "I am army, five dollars."

Linda, standing behind me said, "No dollars, only Jesus."

He then looked at Linda and said, "I love you."

Immediately I recalled all I had heard about how they treat women, I sent up one of those arrow prayers, 'Lord, help.' To every one's surprise, including my own, I found myself beginning to sing, joined quickly by the rest of team.

'All over the world the Spirit is moving, all over the world, just as the prophet said it would be.' The people who had gathered to watch the drama, began to laugh, and the soldier began looking sheepishly around, shook his head and staggered off. A Congolese lorry arrived with some equipment and people started chipping away at the cliff side which was of a soft material. Late in the afternoon, we got the news that there was now sufficient space for small vehicles to pass. Just as we got on the way, a van which was the same make and colour as ours, cheekily nipped in front of us. It was now dark and we were advised that it was not safe to travel in the DRC in the dark, but we had no option.

We were about twenty kilometres from Bukavu when at a village, police stopped us and warned us not to proceed because, up ahead there was rebel activity. There had been shooting and people had been killed. Matthew made a few calls and eventually found a safe place to stay, at a local Norwegian Mission. It was scary travelling through jungle-like terrain at night with the thought of rebels in the area. Another early morning; at five thirty a.m., we were again on the road. On the way we came across the vehicles that had been attacked by the rebels. The sight was disturbing, especially on recognising that one of the vehicles was the one which had nipped in front of us.

Later, Matthew learned that up at the scene of the road accident, there had been rebels watching proceedings, gauged the order of vehicles continuing the journey and expecting that the van with the white people, and the hope of many dollars, was still in prospect, and waited at a convenient place to attack. I don't know the truth of that, but it has led me, when I pray for missionaries in the field, to the word of the Psalmist, *"May the Lord answer you when in distress, may the name of the God of Jacob protect you"* (Psalm 20; Verse 1).

After some quick vehicle repairs we were again on the road, this time to a place called Avira. There we experienced the same response to our proclamation of the Gospel truths, with a number of people being consecrated for Kingdom work in that area. Then it was off to Kabila, where some people were seeing white people for the first time. It was here that Matthew had prayed for a man suffering from Aids. He was healed and gave Matthew a plot of land on which to build a Church. Also, the local chief gave us a piece of land to rent, on which vegetables and rice could be grown. In response to the preaching, one man cried out for salvation. He had been a drunkard and his father would have nothing to do with him. Matthew took him to his father, claiming that he was a new creation.

Later we learned that the whole family came to trust in Jesus and the man, now filled with a new Spirit, enrolled in the Bible School and is now the Pastor of a Church. As a reward for my preaching, I received the gift of a live chicken; my farm boy experience came in handy as I gladly accepted it. As we travelled to these places, Matthew's phone was busy with reports of healing miracles. A Lutheran Bishop with a lung problem was healed, a Pastor suffering depression was delivered. We heard that at Kamituga a pastor's wife, who suffered with daily bleeding was cured, and a seriously ill baby had been healed from malaria. Also the young girl we prayed for over in that clinic was completely healed.

After another hazardous journey we arrived at Sange Mapera where I spoke on the text of John 14. Many people were anointed with the power of the Holy Spirit. Back at our base, Matthew got a call from a pastor at Kamituga, telling him that at our meeting, a person called Mark had recorded my message and took it to a house group in Kieteii. In the message I had asked people to place their hand on any areas of pain and trust God to deal with it. After prayer, five Roman Catholics were healed. On our way to a place called Sange Rutanga, we met with a new problem, when on three occasions, we were stopped by police who claimed that our vehicle had too many people on board and demanded money from us. In response we prayed and worshipped God and He showed us favour. After Matthew claimed that he had authority from God to pass, we were allowed to continue our journey.

On arriving, we learned that a storm in the night had destroyed many houses and the Church. But the Church members had erected canopies between trees and set up chairs, so we held Church there. I spoke of the healing power of God through Jesus, mentioning the Leper who said to Jesus, *"If you are willing you can make me clean."* And to hear Jesus say, *"I am willing, be healed,"* (Mark; Chapter 1; Verse 40), and he was. Also, the blind man Bartimaeus, who was given his sight. (Mark; Chapter 10; Verse 46). I was conscious of a Pastor sitting behind me, who had lost his sight. Two memorable things happened at Sange; one was that Hazel's dream came true, as she spoke with the black women, held their black babies in her arms and blessed them.

For some reason I avoided looking at Bernard, the blind Pastor, but, as I was about to give the blessing, someone said, "What about Bernard?" I went over to him, laid my hands on his eyes and prayed over him in the Name of Jesus to receive the healing blessing given to Bartimaeus.

The next day we returned to base at Bukavu , with plans to visit the Pygmees in their forest community. Also to visit a room, where we found eight people eager to learn from the Bible. Their resources were very limited and we were made aware of their great need for Bibles. For various reasons, we were advised not to visit the Pygmees, which I found very disappointing. In response to the poverty and limited resource we gave many of our surplus garments to Matthew. He was very excited about getting my suit and my shoes. He likened it to the gift of Elisha receiving the cloak of authority from Elijah (1 Kings; Chapter 19; Verse 19).

The next day we were on our way home, and with a two-hour delay at the border control we eventually reached Kigali, where we had a restful night in the home of Nicholas and Elsie. We were so exhausted but were pleased that the journey home was free from problems. However, we were greatly encouraged by learning that there was now to be a Fellowship of Christian Healing; Central Africa. We received reports of many healings, two hundred and fifty people giving their life to Christ and being baptised. On 22nd June Bishop Matthew wrote, telling us that every day, people were coming to his home saying they had been healed and touched by the Holy Spirit. We daily thank God that we had heard and obeyed His voice and went to the Congo.

During our visit we spoke to Matthew about having Micro Projects, enabling people to support their families and the Churches. We gave him money for that. We got confirmation that he had bought rice seed, pigs, and even a motor bike for someone to use as a taxi. Now we were getting confirmation that seed and pigs had been bought. On 28th June, we sent out to Matthew the last of the money donated for the mission. We received a letter of thanks and details of how the money was spent. Rent of an office for the Healing Ministry, some to pay for teachers, food for the orphans, medicine for the clinic, sheets of iron for the roof of the Church at Kamituga and a letter for permission to register the New Ministry of Healing Central Africa. Every day the local radio tells news of miracles. We continue to be amazed at how the Lord blessed our visit to the DRC.

A few days later our joy turned to great sadness when we heard of a disaster on the road near to Sange, where a truck carrying fuel went off the road and the fuel caught fire. Two hundred and thirty-two people died, most of them were men, but there were thirty-six women and thirty-one children who perished. Any survivors had third degree burns. The local hospital ran out of medical supplies and many homes were destroyed, leaving many without shelter or food. Many of the victims could not be identified and were buried in two mass graves.

A week later, our sadness was increased, when we learned that Matthew's dad and seven widows, who were preparing the land for the seed we gave them, had lost their lives as they were returning from the field. Matthew's dad was a great help to us, organising the washing of our clothes and cooking meals for us when we were at Bukavu. That day, members of the Sange Church lost twenty-two family members and thirty-eight Church members have third degree burns. What did I say about the enemy? On 13th July, I had a fellowship meal in my home and one thousand six hundred and sixty pounds was donated and sent to help in the disaster.

Another Visit

On Monday 16th July 2012, Les Turner, Linda Ramsay, Avril Stewart, and Jim Rettie left Inverness to travel to Edinburgh as the first stage of their Congo Mission. Thanks to Brussel Airways, we arrived at Kigali Airport in Rwanda on Tuesday evening. We were again blessed by each being allowed forty-six kilograms instead of the usual twenty-three kilograms of luggage in the 'hold' enabling us to take a lot of medical supplies and other materials helpful to Matthew's ministry; as well as presents for himself and his family. After a welcome overnight at Kigali, we set off for Bukavu in the Democratic Republic of the Congo, which was again to be our base for the mission. Again, we were met by the Church choir, much depleted because some had died in the tanker fire. But joyfully, they led us to our accommodation at the Swedish and Norwegian mission houses, which were very comfortable.

Thursday and Friday were taken up with me teaching at the Oasis Church Bible School (twenty-five students). The team were also involved in Services at the local Church where I spoke on the Book of Joshua (which was my theme for the mission) The GRADUATION ceremonies which were grand occasions, were in two parts; Saturday and Sunday. For these occasions, the team was attired in Professor-type robes and mortar boards. We presented each student with a presentation pen with Celtic markings. Matthew had asked for a KEYBOARD, and a donation had been given for that, so we bought one at Bukavu. It was a real highlight when Les presented the KEYBOARD to the local Church.

Monday 23rd saw us on our way to Mwenga, with the choir, following in an open truck with their KEYBOARD. What should have been a four-hour drive turned out to be a six-hour journey. The reason was we came to a bridge over a swollen river which had been severely damaged, and a vehicle was stuck on it. Eventually, some planks of wood and tree trunks were used to lift the vehicle and enable it to cross. When it was our turn we had to leave the car and watch it be guided over the precarious temporary surface. We then, had to follow on foot, with Congolese men helping the women negotiate the damaged girders and moveable logs. The truck carrying the choir was able to drive through the river safely. The tension was increased by the knowledge that it was an area where rebels were constantly active. There was some comfort in seeing Congolese soldiers watching from advantage points and Pakistani troops from NATO mixing with the crowds.

We eventually arrived at a comfortable guest house. We were interested to learn that there was a conference in progress at the Guest House. It was for the parents of children who had been kidnapped and made into Rebel Soldiers. The parents were given the retreat to help them understand the state of mind of their children, to help them to be integrated back into their families and into society.

The next morning, we had a large congregation waiting for us at the local Church. I, drawing from the story of Joshua spoke on the MERCY OF GOD. At the end, the whole congregation lined up for Ministry. We learned later that many people were healed and delivered from evil spirits. We were then off on our journey to Kamatuga, a two to three-hour drive. On the way, we encountered a severe thunder and lightning storm, with heavy rain, which made the roads even more hazardous. On the way, Matthew's Cell phone was busy with word of healings at Mwenga; – two men healed of goitre; – two women, in their mid-twenties who had experienced no periods, were now menstruating, three people with sinusitis, healed. When we got to Kamatuga we learned that fifty people, twenty of them Jehovah Witnesses, had given their lives to the Lord. The local Pastor suggested that they be baptised on the Sunday, but they didn't want to wait that long and were baptised on the Wednesday. "GLORY BE TO GOD".

We were booked into the Roman Catholic Mission House where we had a candlelit supper before enjoying a welcome restful night. On Wednesday, the plan was for us to continue on to Kitutu, (about a two-hour drive) after the meeting at Kamatuga. But owing to impassable road conditions that was not possible. However, some pastors and members of their congregations, knowing the conditions, walked for two days and two nights from Kitutu, to attend the meeting at Kamituga. With them were some orphans from the Jim Rettie orphanage care centre. We were told that some women who had been healed by the Lord on our visit in 2010, were present and it was so encouraging to see them stand or raise their hands in testimony to their healing.

I, continuing the Joshua theme, spoke of Rahab the prostitute and how, as she waited for her promised deliverance, she trusted in the thin scarlet cord she was asked to hang from the window of her home in the wall of Jericho. I likened it to the thin red line that is woven through the history of God's people; representing the blood of Christ. I had brought with me six thin scarlet cords, one for each of the team members, so instead of laying hands on those who came forward for prayer, we touched them with the cords. The results were amazing. As people were touched by the cords, many seemed to be delivered from some demon-type influence. The men were then asked to leave the meeting and Avril and Linda were invited to address the women; they both gave Spirit inspired messages.

One Pastor with ten women from his Church, had walked for ten days and nights to be at the meeting, only to miss it by two hours. Yet he was content to receive a blessing, which he would take to his people who were recovering, and being cared for in the Church, before starting on the long walk back home. Later that day the local pastor came looking for us. He was carrying a large bin bag. He told us that one woman at the meeting was a Satanist and had sacrificed five of her children to Satan. On hearing the message and being touched by the red cord, she repented and cried out to God and called the Pastor to rid her house of all the symbols of Satan worship. He asked what he should do with the bagful and was given the answer; it had to be burned.

The next day we were up early, at seven a.m. to travel back to Bukavu. Owing to the continued thunder and rain, the roads were even worse. More than once, we had to vacate the vehicle to lighten it, as Matthew drove it through what could only be described as trenches of mud, with embankments on either side, the height of the vehicle. Even then, the vehicle got stuck a few times. We were blessed by the help of many Congolese travellers. Then there was that bridge. Not surprisingly bad, as nothing had been done to improve its state. Again, guided, advised and helped by fellow travellers, Matthew nursed the vehicle across, with the team making it precariously on foot. Linda likened it to walking a tightrope. So, the normal six-hour journey took about eight hours. But praise the Lord, we arrived back safely. However, we learned that the truck carrying the choir had got stuck and the members, many of them very young were walking the last few miles. Later we learned that the truck got free and had picked the choir up and took them home safely. Owing to repairs needed on the vehicle, it was late in the day before we set off for Avira.

In contrast with the other roads, these were exceptionally dry, with sand inches deep, making it like driving through snow. A bit tricky, especially at the corners, with sheer drops into what seemed like mile deep gullies. However, at the times that we dared open our eyes, we were blessed with the most spectacular scenery. With valleys sweeping down to silver mountain streams, and mountains soaring as to the heavens; it is a most beautiful country. Every now and again we would see locals trying to forage a living out of the hillside; like many other things in the Congo, it gives a new meaning to hill farming. We arrived there, to find that our rooms booked at the Swedish Mission House had been given to a group of Bishops from the Swedish Church. We had to do with shake down mattresses and moggy nets, with Matthew and Kashumbi kipping down in the kitchen.

During this time Matthew had received a message from his group at Dodoma in Tanzania, to say that whilst they were praying, they had received word that the people from Scotland were like Joshua. We were greatly encouraged by that. All the time, Matthew was getting messages about healings, at Kamatuga – two women healed of HIV and three husbands had received Jesus and had been baptised. We went on to visit what is known as the Kaliba project. We saw, that what two years ago, was a piece of waste land is now a three hectare area comprising rice fields. We were told that during a rainy time when the lake flooded, the workers took from the irrigation trenches in the rice fields, twenty kilograms of fish. How wonderful is that?

Matthew also showed us the building erected to house a Rice Machine (donated by us) which would enable them to treat their own rice ready for the market. We also visited a Rice Machine working nearby. The plan is that money generated from the rice project would help care for the two hundred orphans in the area and to build a Church; the foundation already prepared, with four thousand bricks to hand. He also plans to have a school for the orphans. Matthew is very forward-thinking and he plans to have a restaurant for all the local workers in the rice fields. We also saw the pig project with many piglets scampering about. We were impressed and greatly encouraged by how Matthew had so wisely invested the resources which we, with many supporters, had contributed to those projects.

On the Sunday we led a Service in the Avira Church. The last time we were there it was just a canvas covered area; now there is a lovely Church and a good congregation. From there, we went to Kaliba where we were met by a huge crowd, including many Bishops and Pastors; also about one hundred orphans. My message from Joshua led into the healing power of Jesus, with Linda giving testimony to the healing of a woman with an issue of blood and Les speaking on the RESURRECTION POWER.

There were many healings. Two miracles I would mention; a woman, who had curvature of the upper part of her spine and was hunched over, was set free with her back straight. A Pastor who came in limping badly, received the laying on of hands and was healed. In amazement he kept swinging his leg to prove it. Later, we learned that twenty people received healing, including five children. God is good … We then all proceeded to the foundation of the new Church where, with the reading of Scripture and prayer, and great rejoicing, I had the privilege of laying the foundation stone. With what we had seen on Saturday and experienced on Sunday, Kaliba was a memorable experience. Exhausted, we returned to base at Avira, where there was a consolation in that, the Bishops' conference had ended and instead of the kitchen floor, Matthew and Kashumbi had a room to themselves. God is good.

Our plan was to conduct a Meeting the next day at Sange Mapera, then travel to Bukavu in preparation for departing for Kigali the next morning. On the way to Sange, we saw some more of the Oasis Churches projects; fields of rice and potatoes, and another pig project. We also saw the burned-out shell of the tanker which in 2010 had overturned, and exploded, killing three hundred people, many of them Church members, including Matthew's father. We were again joined by some Pastors; one coming from as far away as Goma. It seemed that many of the families here were extremely poor, but there was an amazing sense of the Holy Spirit in the time of worship. I sensed a deep sadness among the people. I spoke on the subject of Joshua under the ministry of Moses, how he learned to trust God in the most dark and difficult times. We would have wanted to spend more time with the people of Sange, but there was again a sense of haste for us to get going. However, there was time to anoint and we set aside two people who were to be Pastors for that area. The celebration singing was quite amazing.

As we reached the main road we were met by a large crowd of people who were obviously in heated dispute about something. It turned out to be a tribal dispute regarding who was to be the next chief of the area. We were informed that in their anger they had closed the main road leading to Bukavu, and Matthew felt it was safer to return to Avira and wait for the road to be opened. Late at night we learned that the army and the police had cleared the road. But we now had two main problems, one, we were short of water and food, two, how were we to get to Bukavu, four hours away to collect the rest of our luggage, then travel to Kigali in six hours, in time for our six thirty p.m. check in for our flight home.

Matthew's answer was, a) he would get water from the river, (bad idea) and b) we would leave at five a.m., do the four-hour journey in three hours, have a quick turn about at Bukavu, then do the six-hour journey in five hours. At that point I think that most of the team just switched off and gave it all over to our dear Lord to prevail and to provide. Five a.m. and we were on our way. At the trouble spot, we encountered truckloads of army and police packing up after what must have been their night vigil. We saw signs of how the crowd had set fire to the road, using branches and wood. We arrived at Bukavu about eight thirty a.m. With just time for re-packing our bags and saying farewell to our host and staff at the Norwegian Mission Hostel, we were again on our way. After an aggravating delay at the Rwanda border crossing, we, at speed, greater than the road conditions warranted, set off for Kigali. With only one brief roadside comfort break, and to get some cool fruit drinks we just kept going.

We arrived at Kigali Airport just after six thirty p.m., where I became violently sick. It took great persuasion from myself and the team to persuade the airport staff to allow me on the plane. The sickness continued on board the flight to Brussels, and developed into a severe bout of diarrhoea, which lasted with most of the team for ten days. The source of the sickness was traced to the water from the river. Thanks be to God there were no lasting ill-effects.

So, what was it all about? Well, firstly it was a great encouragement to the Congolese people that we made the visit. Many were blessed by our ministry. We want to thank all for their many prayers from which we drew strength and encouragement. THANK YOU ALL. As a Fellowship working with Matthew, there has been established the CHRISTIAN FELLOWSHIP OF HEALING (Central Africa). Through Micro Loans, people have been enabled to purchase sewing machines to start dressmaking businesses. With the necessary materials they have started basket and soap-making projects. Rice fields have been bought and a RICE MACHINE to treat the rice. People have been able to buy pigs – giving them a good means of livelihood, with the surplus going towards establishing and building Churches. Our continued support has enabled Matthew to establish an orphanage at Kititu, where three hundred children are catered for and educated. It has enabled him to build Churches at Kitutu, Sange and Uvira. To help Matthew get around all of those areas, we financed a vehicle for him suitable for the harsh terrain. Having discussed with Matthew, how it was to be used, we were able to leave with him two thousand three hundred dollars.

Matthew 's email today says, that encouraged by our visit, he has seventy-five students enrolled for the new Bible School Class. God is good. Amen.

The Bible School and the Harvest Centre

On our second visit in 2012, we found that Matthew had started a Bible school at Bukavu with about twenty-nine students. On our return home and to encourage Matthew and the students, I began giving a weekly teaching via the internet. After three years, the Reverend David Scott joined me in that work. There are now five Bible schools throughout the area, and at the last end of term there were four hundred students who graduated. Some of the students are illiterate and Matthew, using a tape recording machine costing almost a thousand pounds, operates a tape teaching system. To further encourage the students, we began giving each graduating student a Bible. That was manageable when the numbers were twenty to thirty, but for the last few graduations the numbers have been in the region of three hundred to four hundred. The cost of a Bible was ten dollars, but owing to the high number ordered, we now get them for six dollars.

With three graduations a year, that comes to a lot of money. But we praise God that, through his work and vision for the Bible School and the Harvest Centre, young men are being taken off the

streets and away from rebel activities. One rebel leader and some members of his rebel group were converted when they heard the children singing a gospel song at Kitutu. That fact became known to the President of the

DRC, who invited Matthew to visit and to speak with him. That resulted in gifts of an area of woodland and five brand new power saws to cut down trees to build a Church. Also, a very generous gift of clothing and school materials for the orphanage was made. In addition, students, some of them pastors and Church leaders, have been equipped to preach and to teach the truths of the Gospel which spiritually enriched their congregations.

This is an amazing testimony to the growth of the Oasis Church Bible School, and many Church congregations in the DRC. It is also a testimony to the great vision and Faith of Bishop Matthew and the faithfulness of members of the Fellowship who have captured the vision.

The Response

Dear spiritual father pastor Jim, my dad

I am happy to tell you that I came from Sange and Uvira last night. I received many greetings from people there; they remember you and they have asked me to tell you to come again. The testimony of our Pastor Bernard brings a great revival at Sange; our Churches there had become very small, but we had a good time to share the Word of God and we have baptized about one hundred and sixty-three people, from different areas around Sange. The testimony of Bernard who was blind, is great. After you prayed for him he started to see. Many people have believed and received Jesus as their Saviour. People have stopped me on the way and they say that the God of Oasis Church is a true God. We thank you so much for this great grace for us. We thank our Lord who connected us to you and to the Healing Ministries, Scotland. We bless his wonderful name to connect you to us; Remember the book of Ruth 1; Versus 16 to 17.

The Fellowship wish to continue to support Matthew, and any royalties gained from this book, will be donated for that work, especially through the Bible Schools and the spread of God's Word in the DRC. **I wish to thank all who have in the past contributed so generously to this mission work in the Congo**; also, the Blythswood organisation for their help and support.

Now My Story

On OCTOBER 24, 2012, I was COMING OUT OF MORRI-SONS SUPERMARKET, when I COLLAPSED WITH a HEART ATTACK. By the grace of God, a highly qualified Paramedic had just driven into the car park. Whilst others were contacting the hospital he attended to me. He testifies to having resuscitated me three times before an ambulance arrived. I was taken to Raigmore Hospital where highly skilled medical staff set about keeping me alive. After some hours of working on me, they realised that whilst my body was responding to the various machines attached to me, I was brain dead.

During that time, my two daughters and members of my ministry team had arrived. The words spoken to my daughters were, "We can do no more for your dad, we can only now apply the Liverpool plan, (make him comfortable and wait for the end), so we are going to remove the support machines and just leave him."

Whilst that consultation was going on, members of the Ministry team were allowed to be with me in the room where I had been set apart. I was later told that their approach was to pray against the diagnoses. Part of their cry was, "O Lord this cannot be, we know this man's programme, and he has much yet to do for you and your Kingdom." The team went home, and later one of the consultants and the Hospital Chaplain, Reverend Derek Brown came into the room and Derek asked the consultant if he could pray over me, and she agreed. And Derek said what he terms a simple prayer, and to their amazement I opened my eyes, wanted to sit up, and was asking for toast. I understand that it caused quite a stir amongst the medical staff, but great joy to family and friends.

I was then taken to a ward and as I watched and waited and I tried to respond to the excellent attention received from the medical staff, I came to realise that they were more concerned for my brain, rather than my body. I was later told that there was much amusement at the answers I gave to some of the many questions. I learned later that as I had been without oxygen for something like forty minutes that they were surprised that I could remember anything. Very few people survive mentally after such a long time without oxygen. Gradually, my memory came back, and it was decided to fit me with a defibrillator, which was implanted into my chest.

My deep concern was about what had been happening spiritually. There were no shining lights, no sign of heaven or the risen, ascended and glorified Lord, no angels to welcome me. Instead, I met with the most horrible looking creatures, worse than any of you might see in the worst horror film; black, slimy creatures with tentacles reaching out to grab me. But just as they were about to grab me there came what I can only describe as an awesome power; like an unseen hand pushing them away. And that happened a few times, but each time that unseen hand brushed the creatures aside. You can imagine how that troubled me more than my physical condition. But I was somewhat comforted in realising that it was the awesome power of the hand of God protecting me in the dark shadow of hell.

It seemed that those precious words of the twenty third Psalm had become real for me; *"Even though I walk through the valley of the shadow of death, I will fear no evil for Thou art with me."* Alongside that I also remembered the words of Jesus who warned that not everyone who says to me, *"Lord, Lord or perform miracles will enter the kingdom of heaven, but only he who does the will of my father who is in heaven"* (Matthew; Chapter 7; Verse 21). Whilst wrestling with that I must have fallen asleep. When I awoke I found a piece of paper on my bed. The writing on it was headed –*A DEEPER TRANSFORMATION*—followed by these words – *"The Spirit of*

the Lord is on you. You are fearfully and wonderfully made. I am speak-
ing to your heart. I am bringing you into alignment with these truths,
spoken in My Word. I am speaking to you about My truth and My heart
for you in the midst of pain and confusion. You are fearfully and wonder-
fully made. You are one whom My Spirit is on, if I am the Lord of your
life and if I reign in your heart. Yet I am seeking after you. I am longing
to go deeper into who you are and transform you ever further. Will you
allow Me to come in and go deeper? Will you choose to exchange your
mere longing for an infilling of more of me? Set yourself apart for Me.
Set your heart apart for Me – Allow Me to come in and bring that align-
ment with My Spirit and My truth." Isaiah 6; (Chapter 1; Verse 1) –
"The Spirit of the sovereign lord is on me, because the Lord has anointed
me to proclaim the good news to the poor." Psalm 139; Verse 14 – *"I*
praise you because I am fearfully and wonderfully made; your works are
wonderful. I know that full well."

In my arrogance, I looked, and I thought only of the first and last
parts of that prophecy. I thought that the Lord must have some
greater things for me to do for Him. The experience I had was
an assurance of the awesome power of the Lord to do whatever
it was He had for me to do. I got really puffed up about being
reminded that I was fearfully and wonderfully made, and have
confirmation of my call to preach the good news with a fresh
sense of God's power.

There was great joy as I spent the Christmas celebrations with
my family at Kinross. Then I went on to spend the New Year
with Angela and Graham at Thurso. On Sunday, we planned to
attend St. Andrew's and St. Peter's Church in Thurso, but got
the time wrong. But on the way, we had passed the West Church
where the congregation were gathering, so we went there. It was
a retired minister who was conducting the Service. As he introduced his text for the message, I nearly fell off my seat. It was
from Hebrews (Chapter 11; Verse 12), *"And so from this one man,*
and he as good as dead, came descendants as numerous as the stars in the
sky and as countless as the sand on the shore." Of course, those words

referred to Abraham, the father of the faith, who went on to establish the greatest faith community the world has ever known.

As the minister spoke into the text, I became convinced that the Lord was speaking to me and He still had great things for me to do for His Kingdom. I was encouraged to believe that the Lord had guided us to be in that Church so that I would have that confirmation. It was one of those 'WOW' situations.

The next day, which was 31 December, Hogmanay, Angela and I were doing some last-minute shopping in Thurso. Walking up the street on the way home, without any warning my defibrillator kicked in with a kick like a mule. I found myself lying on the pavement. On reflection, it is not the most acceptable sight to see a minister of the Gospel, lying on the pavement in a Highland town, on a Hogmanay day. When I got to my feet, Angela, despite the shock of it all got me into a shop and called the ambulance.

When the paramedics arrived, they made their customary checks, one of them said, "From my machines, I am getting readings more like that of a man half your age." I was taken to the local hospital and given the all clear and allowed to get on with my New Year plans.

However, the experience took a lot of the 'wind out of my sails', as they say. Arriving back home, I was faced with the question. What was that all about? Seeking an answer, I was led to look again at the words of the prophecy and what was central to it. Remember what it said – *"You are one on whom My Spirit is on, if I am the Lord of your life and if I reign in your heart. Yet I am seeking after you. I am longing to go deeper into who you are and transform you ever further. Will you allow Me to come in and go deeper? Will you choose to exchange your mere longing for an infilling of more of me? Set yourself apart for Me. Set your heart apart for Me – Allow Me to come in and bring that alignment with My Spirit and My truth."* I realised that I had missed the important part.

That word "if" jumped out at me – **If** I am Lord of your life, **if** I reign in your heart. Of course, there was that section which spoke of what God wanted to, nay, longed to do for me. Finishing with what was my part in receiving that blessing; *"Set yourself apart for Me, set your heart apart for Me, allow Me to come in."* In obedience I set aside four to six hours of the next forty days, pouring over, and searching God's word for guidance and direction, also referring to the book entitled, 'The More Excellent Way' by Henry Wright.

In allowing the Lord to search my heart, I was faced with the awful truth that my heart was full of pride. I came to realise the destructive things that flow out from a heart of pride, things like selfishness, envy, arrogance, being judgmental, greed, power seeking and so many other sinful traits. One example came clearly to my mind, where I would often say that I was the least of God's servants, but in my heart, I believed that no one could do things as well as myself. The Book of Proverbs warns about pride. (Chapters 8 to 13) "God hates pride;" (Chapters 13 to 10) "Pride leads to quarrels;" (Chapters 16 to 18) "Pride goes before destruction;" (Chapters 23 to 29) "A man's pride brings him low." I became convinced that those tentacles reaching out from those awful creatures represented the sinful pride in my heart and God wanted to change that. And the only effective way of dealing with any sin is; first, recognise it; second, take responsibility for it; third, repent of it (before God); fourthly, remove it, resist it and where possible, make restoration. Realising that, I spent quite a time contacting those I knew, whom I had intentionally or unintentionally hurt or let down, and sought their forgiveness.

As I continued to ponder how I was to go on with my work for the Lord and what was to be my future, I was led to consider one by the name of King Hezekiah whose work for God is recorded in 2 Chronicles. In Chapter 29, we are told that he became king at the age of twenty-five. In Chapter 30, God called the people to return to the Lord their God, with verse 8 telling us that he had a heart for the marginalised. There follows a record of Hezekiah's good deeds. Then in 2 Kings, Chapter 20, we are told that he became ill, and God sent the prophet Isaiah to tell Hezekiah that he had better get his house in order, for he was going to die and would not recover. With that Hezekiah turned his face to the wall and prayed to the Lord, reminding God of all his righteous works. In verse 5 Isaiah is sent back with the message from God; "*I have heard your prayer and seen your tears. I will heal you, and add fifteen years to your life;*" I can identify with King Hezekiah, and I constantly claim that promise of fifteen years and hopefully more. I have already enjoyed five years of them. Praise the Lord. And with a fresh sense of God's awesome power and what I have been called to do, I have and hopefully will continue with God's Kingdom work.

It is encouraging that as I continued to preach and to teach, members of the 'ministry team' recognised the effects of the fresh anointing of Spirit and truth. I am also encouraged to believe that the Spirit is moving in the Highlands in a special way. There are now many Churches and fellowships who offer Divine Healing as part of their worship. I still hold on to that vision; that in every Church and meeting of God's people where the Word of God is preached with the power and authority promised by Jesus, that there will be the offer of Healing (Matthew 10). The ministry of Healing on the streets is on the increase, Street Pastors are part of that spiritual outreach. One day, I was speaking at a Christian Fellowship in the Highlands and was speaking on the PROMISE, the PERSUASION and the POWER of the Holy Spirit. Ten people responded to the invitation for prayer.

One woman came forward and said that she just wanted to give thanks to the Lord for the healing she received. She said, "For some time I have suffered severe pain caused by Rheumatoid Arthritis. Last night, I was at a social and could not even get up to dance. Today, I was sitting in my seat and as you spoke, something like a bolt of lightning struck me and I slumped forward. When I straightened up, the pain was gone." Praise the Lord.

I was again at the Fellowship the following Sunday and the woman, full of the joy of the Lord told me that she had been on two occasions, dancing free from pain. In two weeks' time she was going with the Local Scout group to a camp in the Alps, expecting to do some climbing. How wonderful is that? It is so exciting and humbling to see the Word of God live. Does it not say in Psalm 107 (Verse 20); *"He sent forth His Word and healed them."*

Another of the ten was a woman who had a growth or a lump on her body. Linda and I laid hands on her and I learned on the following Sunday that the lump had gone. She was on holiday, so I did not speak to her personally, but members of the Fellowship confirm that it is so. I constantly claim that parting promise of Jesus, recorded in Mark (Chapter 16; Verse 18)*, "In my name they will place their hands on sick people and they will get well."*

Deliverance

After my experience with the student at Aberdeen University, it will not be surprising that a great deal of my Ministry involves the MINISTRY OF DELIVERANCE. I insist that any, who are led to be part of the Ministry Team, have a teaching on the Ministry of Deliverance. I do that as we may be called to what seems a physical or an emotional problem and whilst ministering, a demon may manifest itself, at times without much warning. I used to think that I was well equipped for ministry if I had my Bible with me and that is true. But a well-equipped member of a Healing Ministry Team needs also the assurance that we have the VICTORY over the enemy. I am often called to homes where there is a disagreeable presence (Poltergeist). One of the first things I usually do is read a scripture, such as Revelation (Chapter 12; Verses 10 to 12).

I acknowledge that they are spirits without a body, but they have ears to hear. On hearing words such as those, they know that they must go. The rest is fairly easy. Another thing I often do, is to light a candle, claiming the scripture truth that the darkness cannot overcome the LIGHT. I can watch the light of a candle, and I know where a demon is, what it is about and when it leaves. In Matthew (Chapter 12; Verses 43 and 44), we are warned that if the door is not closed, the demons return with some of their 'buddies'. To prevent the demon from returning we often anoint the doors and windows with oil. So, the well-equipped team member is equipped with a Bible, the assurance of Authority, a candle, and something to light it with, oil, and tissues (for the tears which are often many) and lastly mint pan drops to keep breath clean when praying over someone. But more than that, it is important for us to constantly review our relationship with the Lord.

The teaching in Acts Chapter 19 reveals that it is very dangerous to attempt deliverance based on a second-hand faith. The sons of the priest Sceva discovered that to their awful cost. But one's faith can be greatly tested. One time of testing is when I get a call from someone claiming to be at the end of his or her tether and threatening suicide. Away back at Culloden, I found a peculiar answer when late one Saturday evening as I was putting the last touches to my message for Church the next day, I received a call from a man making such a claim.

After briefly speaking to him on the phone, I found myself saying, "Look, if you could put it off till tomorrow I will come and see you." Was that not a very peculiar response to such a desperate situation? Yet I felt comfortable with it.

The next day, I did visit the man and I spoke to him about Jesus; the man who came to give us life in all its fullness (John; Chapter 10; Verse 10.) I don't know if it was that truth, or the shock of my response the night before, but the man went on to that fullness of life, with much of it spent in the Church. Since then, I have had many such cries for help, usually late at night and given the same response. Praise God I have not as yet lost one. And it left me with an openness to the peculiar ways whereby God sometimes uses us to bring about his purposes.

I think of what I call the monkey story. One day, I got a call from a minister from a Highland town saying that one of his congregation had an unwanted presence in the home. Would I go and deal with it. I said that I would, only if he accompanied me, to which he agreed. I take that approach as ministers need to experience these things. I arranged for team members to be at the appointed time and the appointed place. I had Ruth from Inverness travelling with me, and Hazel, from further north met us at the place, with the minister. The woman of the house ushered us into a room which was her son's bedroom. It was like going into an icebox and it was empty. She explained that her son could not bear to be in the room and he used his sister's room. I set about doing what I usually do; read scripture, light a candle and pray against whatever was causing the problem. Having tried everything.

I was about to give up and suggest that we come at it some other time, when Ruth, standing beside me, said, "This may sound very silly, but when we were driving from Inverness, I was quietly praying that the Lord would show or tell us what to do and I heard the words, 'look for the monkey'." Now, I have difficulty finding words to explain how I felt at that moment.

Here I am, desperately trying to deal with this very serious situation and someone says, "Look for the monkey." But I trust my team, and I believed that it came from the Lord, so I said to the woman, "Does that make sense?"

She replied, "Oh yes, he loves monkeys and has so many stuffed monkeys."

On asking where they were, she told us they would be in his sister's room. I asked her to get them. She came back with her arms full of stuffed monkeys. As I touched each one I commanded any evil spirit to leave, but got no sense of any evil spirit being present. Much deflated in my spirit, my eye fixed on a door in the room and I asked her what it was.

She replied, "It is a cupboard and it will be like a glory hole, as he keeps all his junk there?"

I asked her to open it, and as she did, we saw glaring out at us the ugliest big stuffed monkey. From its eyes, I got all the usual vibes I get when faced with evil forces. I asked the woman where the son had got it and she said that he got it from his granny who brought it home from a holiday abroad, but he didn't really like it, hence it being in the cupboard.

I said to her, "It has to go."

She quickly replied, "I'll give it back to his granny."

I said, "Why would you want granny to have such a thing? It has to go and be burned."

She accepted, and I took it, and in the Name of Jesus, I commanded the evil presence to go out of it, and the room and house, to be dealt with by Jesus. I then asked Hazel to place it outside the door of the house. As she did so, the room began warming up to a normal temperature. But the story doesn't end there, as I asked Hazel to take the monkey home and burn it. Hazel is a farmer's wife and on the farm, they have a large drum that is used as a small incinerator. Hazel put the monkey in the drum, added a little fuel and put in the fire. She got the shock of her life when the monkey seemed to explode, causing her to run to the house. Watching from her kitchen window, she witnessed an atomic like plume of black filthy smoke, which lasted longer than normal. Such happenings can be a bit scary. That is why it is important for those involved, to be sure of the victory we have in Christ and however foolish it may seem, be guided by the Lord.

The Vision and the Painting

Recently, I attended a Christian Conference in Morayshire, Scotland, given the title 'Refuel'. One morning, whilst listening to the guest speaker, I noticed a young artist sitting at the end of the platform. She was painting onto her canvas what the Spirit was saying to her. At one point, I looked over to where she was working, and I nearly fell off my seat. Her painting was developing to be the exact picture of the vision I saw of the Risen Lord Jesus, way back in that meeting in the Church in Edinburgh, twenty-five years before. I believe that the painting was to remind me of that vision and experience which renewed and empowered my ministry so long ago.

At the end of the meeting I, much overwhelmed, went to speak with the artist, intending to encourage her. Hazel, one my ministry team who realised the impact the painting had on me, joined us. Later, I learned that Hazel had bought the painting for me. It now has a prominent place in my home. A place where I see it when I get up in the morning and when I go to bed at night. It is good to be reminded that the Lord continually refuels us with His Spirit and encourages us to continue in His Service.

As I write this, I hear that owing to a lack of staff, space and money, the National Health Service (NHS) are struggling to meet the needs of the sick. I am bold enough to suggest that, if the Christian community were more aware of and open to the healing power of Jesus, the NHS load could be lessened.

Often, when I am in the midst of it all and see God at work in such amazing ways, I find myself saying, "Is this the uneducated farm boy, with a wayward past, whom God is using to advance His Kingdom?" If God, by His grace and mercy would use one such as myself in His Kingdom work, there is hope for everyone. I pray that wherever we go and witness we will know the blessing of His Word "And the power of the Lord was present for Him to heal the sick." (Luke Cpt 5 V 17.)

The author

The Reverend James Rettie was born in 1935 in
Aberdeen and lives in Inverness Scotland. He is a
retired Minister Of The Gospel and leader of The
Ministry Of Divine Healing. He is a widower with
two daughters, two granddaughters and two great
granddaughters. He first trained as a missionary
serving the Home Board of the Church of Scotland.
He established a congregation at the Barn Church,
Culloden, Inverness. He went on to train for the
Ministry of Word and Sacrament. He served his
probationary period as a Minister in the Presbytery
of Lanark and thereafter as Minister of Melness
and Tongue Church in Sutherland. Then he was
led into the Ministry of Divine Healing which after
retirement, took him to places like Malawi, South
Africa and the DRC. His favourite activities are
fishing, teaching and preaching.